The Revd Dr Cally Hammond is the Dean of Gonville and Caius College, Cambridge. She began her academic life as a classicist, first at Oxford and then at Cambridge, where her research on the Roman historians taught her the value of stories and narratives as a way of communicating truths and beliefs. This has stood her in good stead when thinking about the Gospels and the early Church. As well as working in academic life in Oxford and Cambridge, she spent seven years in full-time ministry in rural parishes in the diocese of Ely. She is the author of *Passionate Christianity: A journey to the cross* (SPCK, 2007).

JOYFUL CHRISTIANITY

Finding Jesus in the world

Cally Hammond

First published in Great Britain in 2009

Society for Promoting Christian Knowledge
36 Causton Street
London SW1P 4ST

British Library Cataloguing-in-Publication Data
A catalogue record for this book is available from the British Library

ISBN 978-0-281-06087-0

1 3 5 7 9 10 8 6 4 2

Typeset by Graphicraft Limited, Hong Kong
Printed in Great Britain by Ashford Colour Press

Produced on paper from sustainable forests

*To the people of the parishes of St Mary the Virgin,
Gamlingay, with Hatley St George and East Hatley,
and St Mary, Everton-cum-Tetworth, with gratitude*

Contents

———◆———

Introduction

—·•·—

Galatians 4.4–5
But when the time had fully come, God sent forth his Son, born of woman, born under the law, to redeem those who were under the law, so that we might receive adoption as sons.

John 1.14
And the Word became flesh and dwelt among us, full of grace and truth; we have beheld his glory, glory as of the only Son from the Father.

Why do we believe in God? There may be countless ways to answer this question, but one thing is plain. It is not because we have many direct experiences of his presence, or are sure what he wills for us, that most of us believe. Of course there are Christians who insist that they know exactly what God wants them to do, and to be. Most of us, though, make no such claims. We are wary of identifying what *we* want with what God wills for all humankind, or even our local Christian community – never mind for us as individuals. Instead, we tend to rely on a complexity of factors, the rich variety of our life experiences, which we do not feel obliged to dissect in a hunt to pin down divine messages. There is the haze of our imprinted memories, layering poetry upon story, and story upon the raw data of human experience. Faith is something we don't necessarily think of as needing analysis. Instead we can simply *inhabit* it, like a comfortable, familiar place. When we come home after dark, and enter without switching on every light, we may not be able to see what is around us very clearly, but we can navigate our way with confidence. So too with faith: it is not that we turn our back upon sense experience, only that we have recognized its limitations in expressing what we think is really worth expressing.

Faith may not be founded upon articulate reason, or dependent upon sensory data, yet belief in God continues to be the foundation of our harmonious existence in the world. This way of describing the day-to-day state of our belief in God may seem like a rejection of 'real' knowledge, a deliberate flying in the face of the plain facts of science, a wilful refusal to set aside the fantasies of childhood for a greater and more lasting kind of truth. Yet believers, no less than scientists (and the two categories are not mutually exclusive), are eager for clarity, for some evidence that their intuitions about the divine are on the right track, even if not conclusively or demonstrably true. Apart from those few who are privileged with a direct revelation (or who think that they have a direct line to the Almighty), those of us who express belief in God are dependent on the same sources as the millions who have gone before us for finding out what God wants from us:

- Scripture
- tradition
- worship
- the world
- prayer.

These five sources provide all our knowledge and belief about God. Scripture tells stories of God's interactions with the human past; to be specific, it does so by means of *significant* stories – stories which are preserved and privileged as communicators of meaning beneath the everyday occurrences of human living. Tradition shows how faith communities have taken those scriptural records of the past and applied them in ways which shape the human present, and the future. Worship works more at the microcosmic level – it is a means of imprinting eternity onto time (as in the repeated rites and ceremonies of the Church's year), and newness of life onto ancient patterns of behaviour and thought, within individual communities of believers. The world, according to some Christians, is not a reliable source of knowledge about God at all. They argue that the world has nothing to tell us about divine truth, and that the only reliable way for God to make himself known to us is through direct revelation. Such revelation is experienced in prayer, then preserved in Scripture and tradition, and finally communicated in worship. But now that global warming and threats to our planet's future from misuse of its resources are confronting us more and more insistently, Christians are being challenged to rethink their ideas, and to see the very work of creation itself as a divine act of self-disclosure. How to read and understand the world in which we live – *that* is one of the tasks before us. As for prayer, all that need be said now is that it is a means of communication with the divine; and that even the desire to pray is an opening up of ourselves to the infinite possibilities of God.

These five sources of truth are always open to exploration. They contain a rich variety of practice and understanding, and yet each has its own significance for us at the individual level. The balance between the five differs from Christian to Christian, according to our denomination, personality, priorities and situation in life. When we think of the five together, the task of understanding why we choose to express belief becomes less daunting. Besides, we are not alone. If religion is a delusion, it is a very big one. We do not need to begin by feeling discouraged, or by being tormented by the suspicion that our beliefs are only a venerable type of wishful thinking. Scripture, tradition, worship, the world and prayer are things which all appeal directly to the world of sense experience. They are grounded on memory and fact, on places and buildings and people and moments in time. Or at least the first four are. Prayer as a category needs a different approach, because in prayer we set aside externals, and open ourselves to the divine presence directly.

Christianity has always seen itself as a historical faith. The early Christian teachers emphasized this fact to encourage new Christians to believe that they were putting their trust in something reliable. They used creeds (among other things) to emphasize the historical reality of the Christian story. The statement in the creeds that Jesus was 'born of the Virgin Mary' is there precisely to underline that historical reality of God entering not just into the human world, but also the human mode of existence. The mention of Pontius Pilate in the Nicene and Apostles' Creeds, moreover, ties the earthly life of Jesus of Nazareth to a moment in history which can be acknowledged *from outside the context of faith*. Christianity has always been concerned with how it appeared to those outside the faith, because it has always cared about how those outside the faith might be encouraged to become those *inside* the faith.

The historical reliability of Christianity is constantly being challenged. In the nineteenth century it was the publication of Darwin's *The Origin of Species* (1859) which caused the biggest shockwaves. The more disturbing challenge in the long term probably came from the slow 'drip, drip' of the new critical thinking on the Bible, which unsettled people's beliefs that the Scriptures were simple history, or a straightforward account of what had happened in the past. Those who had long ago written the texts which came to be sacred Scriptures first for Jews, and then for Christians, had not thought that they were writing about how the world actually came into being, or predicting the distant future of their faith. But for many centuries their writings had been read as if this was precisely what they *had* been doing. So when scholars started to uncover gaps between what the Bible said, and what archaeology told them, the result-ing crisis of confidence among Christians was profound. From the sense that one had to choose between the Scriptures and the brain, between the witness of sacred text and the application of one's intelligence, was generated the modern divide between fundamentalist and liberal Christians.

The reactions of the churches both to Darwin and to the new historical attitude to the Bible show how profound was the challenge to the religious status quo which both had evoked. What is more, they also showed (not for the first or last time) how easily ignorance and fear in the churches could turn Christians into agents of their own destruction. Among current challenges to 'ordinary' faith today are Richard Dawkins and Dan Brown, both of whom, in their different ways, have picked up charges being laid against the Christian faith from earliest times, that it is either delusional or a perversion of historical reality.

Unlike the millions who have gone before us, we are not living any more in a culture which accords automatic respect to tradition. The fact that something has always been believed or done, or that it has always been believed or done *like this*, no longer encourages us to trust in it, or regard it with reverence. In respect of religious belief, which makes demands without guaranteeing results, our default setting has recently been firmly switched to 'off'. Religious belief is now under attack as never before. In the western world we are witnessing a clash not between rival religious views, but between religion and non-religion, belief and atheism. This is not for the first time, of course. The rise of Marxist belief systems privileged atheism over theism, but in an ideological way; that is different from the kind of atheism which is based on indifference and rootless-ness. Down the centuries Christianity had been able to assume that even if its core beliefs in the incarnation, atonement and resurrection were not shared, the common assumption under-pinning them all – the existence of God – did find wide accep-tance. The argument then was not about whether we believed, but *what kind of a God we believed in*.

All that has changed, in the developed world at least. In the public sphere the real debate is no longer between Jew or Muslim and Christian, or Catholic and Protestant. It is between faith and atheism, or, putting it more polemically, between believing in God and believing in nothing (except perhaps in ourselves). The tools formerly developed by Christians for explaining and defending their faith both to outsiders and to those within, simply do not work when applied to the clash between faith and atheism. This can leave Christians in dif-ficulty, wondering whether in fact their faith does make sense at all; and what to do about the convictions which continue to rule their lives, when they seem to have lost their credibility.

The Christian doctrine of the incarnation is, to many, a problem. It seems to involve making claims which are too big even for the most conceited of religions, about the degree to which God is involved in human affairs. Also, it undermines what much prejudice against religion is grounded on, namely the belief that God rules as a (mostly) benevolent despot over cowering humanity. At the other end of the problem-spectrum is another difficulty with the incarnation – that it could appear to be a kind of idolatry, in which believing in an incarnate God is just another way of worshipping ourselves. Those who know about the way the doctrine of the incarnation developed will also be aware of the risks of doing spiritual gymnastics, divid-ing the incarnate Christ into human and divine in a way which could seem to make nonsense of the wholeness of every human person, not just that of Jesus of Nazareth.

So we suffer from a lack of confidence about the intellectual foundations of our faith. One option is to take refuge in funda-mentalism; but this is not for the majority, who are looking for a way to combine understanding and faith, not divorce them. What emerges from this crisis of confidence is that we have not turned our back on religious belief at all; but we *have* lost confidence that we understand what kind of a thing our religious belief is, and ought to be. Is it a moral or ethical system? a form of magic (i.e. a means of controlling the environment by means of secret formulae)? a psychological phenomenon? a kind of mass hysteria? a comfort blanket of delusional certainty in a changing world? The aim of this book is to work out what kind of a thing our Christian belief is, by making use of an ancient prayer called the 'joyful mysteries'. Within this prayer we shall uncover a 'spiritual matrix' for human growth and development in the faith, which will help us to see the hand of God at work in the everyday moments of our lives. That matrix, or pattern, will reveal how we can live out the Christian life by finding our vocation in community and family.

It is an urgent task. The uncovering of this spiritual matrix should provide a framework for building confidence among Christians in the fullest, broadest meaning of the incarnational faith we celebrate each Christmas. After all, the incarnation, with all its implications for our common life, is the doctrine which says most to us, and in a form we ought to be able to understand, about who and what God is, and who and what we are. And Christmas highlights, like nothing else, the gap between our idealized images of ourselves as individuals, families and communities, and the reality of the pressures we face, through this crisis of confidence which besets us.

If 'joyful Christianity' means anything, it means living a faith which is brimming with *confidence*. To show how we can find this kind of confidence in faith, we shall explore the 'joyful mysteries', through which Christians have long reflected on key moments in the life of Jesus, and use them to see how God is at work in our everyday lives. The five joyful mysteries are:

- the annunciation (Luke 1.26–38)
- the visitation (Luke 1.39–56)
- the nativity (Luke 2.1–21)
- the presentation in the Temple (Luke 2.22–40)
- the finding in the Temple (Luke 2.41–52).

There is so much for us to absorb when we think about the Christian Christmas, and the meaning of the Bible stories about Jesus' birth which we know so well and love so dearly, that we need to focus on key details. Each of the five mysteries makes its own contribution to that central Christian doctrine we call 'incarnation'. It is a word so familiar to Christians that they barely notice either how little they understand it, how extraordinary is its message about the God they believe in.

The prayer called the joyful mysteries sheds light on what the incarnation means, because, just like Scripture, tradition, worship and the world around us, prayer is a source of knowledge about God. Such prayer is set apart from these other sources of understanding, though. Not because it requires great skill or long practice (although both these things will help) but because it comes closest to allowing us an unmediated access to God's will and being (no words, no texts, no structures between God and us). If prayer means being open to the possibility of God, there is no pretence of objectivity in this exercise. There is no such thing as objectivity about God. Everyone has a point of view. So the joyful mysteries can add something, through prayer, to the evidence at our disposal when we consider the matter of belief in an incarnate God.

This book is for those who want to understand what they believe, and who are also prepared to accept the limitations of human understanding. It is not for those who are seeking straightforward reassurance about the historical events of Jesus' conception and nativity, or his childhood. It is intended either for individual reading or for group study, and can be used at any time of year, but it will be especially helpful across Advent and Christmas, using the first three mysteries to prepare for Christmas Day, and the last two to reflect on it afterwards. When I looked at another traditional prayer, the sorrowful mysteries, in my earlier book, *Passionate Christianity* (SPCK, 2007), I showed how they come to their climax with the final mystery, the crucifixion; but the shape of the joyful mysteries is quite different – the focus is on the central mystery of the five, namely the *nativity*. This makes the experience of praying the joyful mysteries feel quite different from the sorrowful mysteries of the Passion, and not just because of their contrasting factual content. Everything is focused on the moment when the Word was born into the world as a human being, a helpless baby, in poverty and obscurity.

When people pray the joyful mysteries, they usually take a scene from the Gospel (in this book, we shall be using St Luke), and imagine themselves as part of it, involved in it as one of the characters, or even as part of the scenery. What we discover when we do this is that the Bible story of Christmas, like all the Bible, is centred on *relationships* – our relationship with God, and, flowing from that, our relationships with one another; our relationships with the past from which we have grown, and with the future which is our gift to generations yet to come. In the sorrowful mysteries of the Passion, Jesus is a lonely figure; but in the joyful mysteries of Christmas, we see Jesus as part of a family and a community. Here, then, is a chance to find out how we relate to Jesus through our relationships with the people who share their lives with us – our family, friends, neighbours and colleagues.

So what is this joyful Christianity which we claim, and try, and want to believe in? We take the first step into these mysteries, trusting that somewhere within them is a fundamental truth about us, and about God. As we do so, we walk in hope that if old certainties are left behind, whatever takes their place will be still deeper, richer and more powerful, as we begin to see more clearly than before what is the breadth and length and height and depth, and to know the love of Christ that surpasses knowledge, so that we may be filled with all the fullness of God (Ephesians 3.18).

Upon Christ's Nativity

Now in a manger lies the eternal Word:
The Word He is, yet can no speech afford;
He is the Bread of Life, yet hungry lies;
The Living Fountain, yet for drink He cries;
He cannot help or clothe Himself at need
Who did the lilies clothe and ravens feed;
He is the Light of Lights, yet now doth shroud
His glory with our nature as a cloud.
He came to us a Little One, that we
Like little children might in malice be;
Little He is, and wrapped in clouts, lest He
Might strike us dead if clothed with majesty.
Christ had four beds and those not soft nor brave:
The Virgin's womb, the manger, cross, and grave.
The angels sing this day, and so will I
That have more reason to be glad than they.

Rowland Watkyns (1610–1664)

1

The annunciation

———•◆•———

In the sixth month the angel Gabriel was sent from God to
a city of Galilee named Nazareth, to a virgin betrothed to a
man whose name was Joseph, of the house of David; and the
virgin's name was Mary. And he came to her and said, 'Hail,
O favoured one, the Lord is with you!' But she was greatly
troubled at the saying, and considered in her mind what sort
of greeting this might be. And the angel said to her, 'Do not
be afraid, Mary, for you have found favour with God. And
behold, you will conceive in your womb and bear a son, and
you shall call his name Jesus. He will be great, and will be
called the Son of the Most High; and the Lord God will give
to him the throne of his father David, and he will reign over
the house of Jacob for ever; and of his kingdom there will be
no end.' And Mary said to the angel, 'How shall this be, since
I have no husband?' And the angel said to her, 'The Holy
Spirit will come upon you, and the power of the Most High
will overshadow you; therefore the child to be born will be
called holy, the Son of God. And behold, your kinswoman
Elizabeth in her old age has also conceived a son; and this is
the sixth month with her who was called barren. For with
God nothing will be impossible.' And Mary said, 'Behold,
I am the handmaid of the Lord; let it be to me according to
your word.' And the angel departed from her.

Every year, when Christmas came round in the parishes where I was Rector, I became – yet again – aware of a big gap in my preaching. Somehow the right moment never came to face it. Every Christmas, with churches full of people who rarely attended, it felt like the wrong moment to pull the threadbare carpet of belief out from under their feet by tackling hard questions about the Gospel stories of the birth of Jesus. We have all read horror stories about vicars ruining Christmas by telling tiny tots there's no such person as Father Christmas; or refusing to sing certain much loved carols because of their dodgy theological content. I shall never forget a well-intentioned parish priest trying to bring home to his congregation at Midnight Mass how dirty the birth of Jesus must have been, with all those *animals* in the stable, all that *mess*, he kept insisting. As we shall see, there is a serious point to be made by imagining how the birth must have taken place, to get across the real meaning of the incarnation. But Midnight Mass and manure don't really mix. That sermon missed the mark.

Or did it? I can't help thinking of Monty Python's film, the *Life of Brian*. Its opening scene – in which the magi arrive in Bethlehem, can't tell exactly which house is directly beneath the star, and give their gifts to the wrong child (Brian) – show just how hard it is to visualize Gospel realities. In our imagining, we tend to draw heavily on images which often have little relationship to the real world of Bible days – but this is no bad thing. The artists whose work adorns our Christmas cards didn't look for authentic historical reality either. They put the Gospel characters in the world of their own day – dressed, living, behaving like themselves. Sometimes they added their own faces to the characters they painted; on one level it's a bit of a cheek, but on another level it says something important about how intimately the Gospel stories of Jesus are connected to our own lives. Our mental map can incorporate elements from pictures we have seen with fragments from our own experience and imagination. Unfortunately, the quality of *imagination*, especially in prayer, is not one which the Church has encouraged much over the years, perhaps because the Church has been more concerned about shutting down what is incorrect than opening up what is possible. But imagination needs to be activated if our prayer life is to flourish.

The joyful mysteries begin with the story of someone just like us. The salvation of God's people hangs upon the life and character of a single human being, and it is crucial to the meaning and power of that story that she has a free choice in everything she did and said. There is no doubt that this woman, Mary, really existed – if the man Jesus existed (as he certainly did), then she must have existed too. If she had not been a real historical person, Jesus might still exist and be real (like, for example, the angel Gabriel), but he could not be *human*.

Thinking about the annunciation means relating the Bible story to what we call the real world. Many people, when they read about it, get stuck on the problem that it seems to present to a scientific generation like our own. There is no point in sidestepping this with pious platitudes. Luke is the only writer to record what happened to Mary, but he does not tell us anything at all about where his information came from. He does refer to many previous writers having recorded the events he is describing, and tells the person for whom his Gospel is written, Theophilus, that his account will record the truth about things Theophilus has already heard of from other sources (1.1–4). Luke is interested in the miraculous nature of the conception as a proof of divine power, and a guarantee of the authenticity of Jesus' ministry. By focusing on Mary's role, rather than Joseph's (as Matthew does), he emphasizes what for him – and for later theological thinkers – was the key point: the authentic humanity of Jesus.

There are two Bible passages which record details of Jesus' ancestry (Matthew 1.1–17; Luke 3.23–38). Both seek to prove, though in different ways, that through Joseph he was a descendant of King David. Luke goes into detail about this with respect to his birth in Bethlehem, as does Matthew. But there is a snag, which is easily spotted: Joseph was not the blood father of this child. He is the adoptive father, or foster-father. Important as he must have been to the infant and the child Jesus, he was not a blood relative. This problem was quickly noticed by the first Christian thinkers, for whom the descent of Jesus from David was essential to his identity as the Lord's Messiah. What could be done?

This apparent problem poses a difficulty for those who would dismiss the virginal conception of Jesus as a historical fiction. True, Paul does not refer to a virginal conception in his letters, and it is not mentioned elsewhere in the New Testament – it was the resurrection of Jesus, not his miraculous conception, which began the search for the meaning of his life as a whole. Yet for Paul and the first Christians, the identity of Jesus the Jew, as the embodiment and fulfilment of God's purposes in calling the Jewish people as his own, is central to the meaning of the cross and resurrection. A non-virginal conception, with Joseph (of the house and lineage of David) as the blood father, would have suited the message more neatly. But still the virginal conception persisted as the true record of his parentage.

So it came about that by the end of the second century, Christian writers like Bishop Irenaeus of Lyons were finding an answer to the problem by arguing that Mary too must have been descended from the line of David. However awkward the virginal conception might be as a stumbling block to belief in the Davidic descent of Jesus, it was not rejected. Naturally, perhaps inevitably, a recognition of the ultimate importance of Jesus pushed people into reflecting on the role of his mother, as the guarantor of his humanity.

Luke presents Mary as a normal human being. She is set within the context of an ordinary human family – Elizabeth and Zechariah are her relations. This is not incidental: it is of the essence of our identity as human beings that we are born of another human being, and not made or manufactured by God. Even the gods of ancient Greece and Rome had to be born, albeit by remarkable methods. The virgin goddess Athena sprang fully armed from her father Zeus's head after he swallowed her mother. Artemis, Apollo and Hercules were the offspring of liaisons between gods and humans. Aphrodite was not born by procreation at all. Such bizarre legends, which run counter to the facts of normal human existence, make the story of the conception of Jesus sound unexpectedly normal by contrast.

For him, as for us, identity comes from our parents. We take it for granted, barely thinking about it, that our identity as human beings is guaranteed by the identity of our parents, and that we can transmit this identity through the children we may have. The gods of the ancient world were distant from humankind, dangerous and extraordinary, both in the manner of their conception and in their behaviour to one another and towards human society. We must not forget how extraordinary is the ordinariness of Jesus' emergence into the world

Our human identity, then, depends on that of our parents, This is what the Bible also indicates, when it uses terms such as 'son of man', or 'man that is born of a woman' – these phrases confirm that to be human is not to be generated out of nothing but to be someone's child. In the story of the creation of humankind in Genesis, only Adam (which is the Hebrew word for a 'man' – he is not given a name in the story) is made, not 'begotten'. He is created out of the dust of the earth, and is earthly, and earthy (1 Corinthians 15.47). Even Eve (which means 'Living') is made of human 'stuff' (Genesis 2.21–23). So the man Jesus had to be conceived and born, and Luke describes the conception in such a way as to insist beyond any doubt that his humanity was real. Still, the *manner* in which it

5

took place is much disputed, because Luke's Gospel is almost the only record we have of how the man Jesus came into the world. There is just the briefest of references in Paul, who says that 'when the time had fully come, God sent forth his Son, born of woman' (Galatians 4.4). His words confirm that Jesus was truly human, but they do not tell us what Paul thought about how Jesus was conceived.

We are comfortable with reacting to the story of Jesus' conception and birth as a symbol for our own life stories – our existence as part of a family, the carrying and bearing of our own children, our hopes for the future of those we love. But science demands that we question the story as Luke tells it. Few Christian writers in the past tried to picture either the conception or the birth of Jesus in literal detail, thinking that it would detract from the mystery if people went into what they regarded as intimate or sordid particulars. Yet birth is no longer something from which men are excluded, so that may soon be changing. The attitude that birth is messy and sordid tells us a lot about why the incarnation of God was such a shocking idea at first, but although birth is no longer a mysterious, wholly female preserve, it has become so medicalized, and removed from the home environment, that its messy normality is still at a distance from everyday life. When women give birth in unexpected places, it makes news, because it shows us a mystery breaking into the realm of the ordinary. We should remember too that giving birth in our society is relatively safe both for mother and baby. In the developed world fewer than 20 children in 1,000 will die before the age of 5 years. Those of us who live in the comfortable security of that developed world, with our safe medical facilities and secure social support structures, should never take that relative safety for granted, either in everyday life or in our reflections on Bible days long ago. Jesus was born in the kind of poverty we see in the developing world, where the number of children who die before the age of five is nearly one in five. Nor is it just the babies who are at risk. Whereas in our society one mother in almost 3,000 will die around childbirth, in poorer countries the risk rockets to 1 in 16. It is easier to sentimentalize pregnancy and birth when it is a relatively safe procedure than when it is a terrifying gamble with life and death.*

The Gospel story is so famous, and so familiar, that it can slip through our mind without us being able to grasp it, and relate it to our own life experience. This is because we usually listen to it at Christmas, a packed and pressurized time. Not that encountering it in the context of worship *detracts* from our ability to understand it: quite the reverse. Worship encapsulates its historical significance, expressing (as solitary reflection alone cannot) the universal meaning. Yet this corporate experience can be too dense in its impact. Better, then, to go back nine months from Christmas Day, to 25 March, the day which used to be commonly known as Lady Day, or the Feast of the Annunciation. Annunciation means 'announcement' – it focuses the meaning on the words of the angel, who is named as Gabriel (Luke 1.19; see Daniel 9.21). His words *announce* God's plan for the young woman – 'you will conceive in your womb and bear a son . . . of his kingdom there will be no end'. The angel's words seem like the important ones here, because they tell Luke's readers what God is doing. Those readers have already seen Gabriel in action, making a similar *announcement* to Zechariah (Luke 1.5–25) – so there is dramatic tension in the waiting for a response. Zechariah failed the test (v. 18); what will Mary say?

There is even more to this story than the revelation of God's purposes. Other words are spoken. Mary's response is first of all something personal; but in the circumstances of her position,

---

* Maternal mortality in 2000: estimates developed by WHO, UNICEF and UNFPA.

it is also paradigmatic. In other words it stands as a symbol for what *our* response to God ought to be. Anyone who knows the Bible well will recognize in this story of the annunciation a familiar pattern – God calls, human beings respond. Other stories from the Bible spring to mind – Abraham (Genesis 12.1), Samuel (1 Samuel 3.4), the prophets (Isaiah 6.8–9; Jeremiah 1.4–10; Ezekiel 1.28—2.7). There are also examples of God making known his choice of people in less direct ways, as in the election of David (1 Samuel 16.6–13). To judge from Scripture, it seems at first glance as if the people concerned have only one choice in such circumstances: to do as God commands. Abraham does not question or argue, he simply gets up and goes, as he has been told to do. But in fact people vary widely in their reactions to God's call, and even when they have chosen to obey the summons, they are not always consistent about it. Isaiah and Jeremiah are more like Moses (Exodus 4.1, 10), reluctant because of their intense awareness that they are not worthy; and in Jeremiah's case, struggling with the burden of malice which comes with proclaiming an unwelcome message (Jeremiah 4.19–31; 14.13; 15.10–12; 18.19; 20.7). He and Ezekiel, like Moses (Exodus 5.22), even complain to God about his commands and choices. Ezekiel bursts out in the end with a reproach for the scorn and disbelief which the prophecies are attracting to him – 'Ah Lord God! they are saying of me, "Is he not a maker of allegories?" ' (20.49).

One prophet, however, goes further even than this – Jonah. When Jonah is first chosen to proclaim the word of the Lord, he runs away (Jonah 1.1–3). When finally he does go to Nineveh, his prophesying succeeds, and the people repent. But then God decides not to destroy the city after all – and Jonah furiously rebukes God for making him look ridiculous (4.1–5). So immediate, unquestioning obedience is certainly not the only option when people in the Bible are faced with a call from God. Within the range of possibilities, from wordless acceptance to passionate rejection, what can we make of the response given in Luke?

- She was greatly troubled. (1.29)
- 'How shall this be?' (1.34)
- 'Behold, I am the handmaid of the Lord; let it be to me according to your word.' (1.38)

Mary's words indicate perplexity, even doubt as to the physical possibility for her to conceive (perhaps a counterpart to Sarah; Genesis 18.12–13). Mary does not confess, though, that she feels herself unfit for the task. She does ask exactly the same question that Zechariah did – *how can this be?* He was struck dumb for doubting. She is not, so there must be something about the manner of her asking, or the meaning behind her question, which is clear to the angel, though not apparent to us. It is, after all, a perfectly reasonable question for both of them to ask – Zechariah knows that he and Elizabeth are too old to become parents in the normal course of nature; and Mary knows that as a virgin she cannot have a child. It is worth remembering that just because modern science had yet to develop, people were not stupid – they knew how babies come into the world.

Mary accepts the call. This unquestioning obedience has been seen as a supreme model for Christians to imitate. Yet it goads us into asking uncomfortable questions about the free will and independence of Mary – was she just a pawn in God's plan? Did she have any say at all in her own future? It prompts us to wonder about how we might react if challenged by a divine calling – would we obey unquestioningly? And in our individualistic generation, it makes us ask how the submerging of our self into the will of God could be a good thing. In other words, we want to know about the moral and theological value of Mary's 'yes' to God. Soft words about obedience will not suffice. We need to dig deeper.

We could argue that back in those days, people did not have such a strongly developed understanding of the unique individuality of the human person. That would mean that the impact of God's election of Mary need only concern us as far as she was necessary to the greater good, the overarching scheme. But Luke's account makes it difficult to maintain this line. He *names* Mary – and names her not once but four times. This cannot be incidental. The first mention of her name is particularly emphatic – 'and the virgin's name was Mary'. The angel (who is also given a name, Gabriel, which means 'God is my hero') drives home that emphasis when he addresses her – 'Do not be afraid, Mary.' Then twice Luke repeats 'Mary said'. It is surprisingly rare for women to be named in either the Old or the New Testament, though Luke is an exception, in the particular emphasis he gives to the role and importance of women in Jesus' ministry. So we can be sure that he has a reason for doing this.

We often read that names are important in the Scriptures, because they carry meaning. Knowledge of a name, and the uttering of it, confers power. Jacob struggles with 'a man' to wrest his name and a blessing out of him (Genesis 32.24–30). God's name is a great secret disclosed to Moses, the leader of his chosen people (Exodus 3.13–14). The mother of Jesus has the same name as the sister of Moses – Miriam (the Hebrew form) or Mariam (the Greek form). Its meaning is not clear, but it may have signified something like 'Excellence'. If this is correct, it certainly adds a layer of meaning to Luke's story. But the primary importance of her naming for Luke is that it anchors his account in a specific historical reality, just like his giving of a date, 'in the sixth month'. It is the same concern to emphasize historical reality which leads to the naming of both Mary and Pontius Pilate in the Apostles' Creed and the Nicene Creed. More important still, it ties the conception of the son of God, the moment when God incarnate became a reality, not only to a moment in time but to a real human individual.

Luke is sometimes known as the first Christian historian, because he wrote not only a Gospel life of Jesus, but also an account of the first beginnings of the Church ('the Acts of the Apostles'). His efforts to ground the story of Jesus' conception and birth in historical time were intended to assure Christians that their faith was based on something which really happened. Greek and Roman religion was mostly a mesh of fable, myth and ritual, conveying meaning but making no claims about history. In this, as in so much else, Christianity stood out from the crowd. Luke did his best with the historical facts as he received them from his sources, and as he understood them. But in a modern historical perspective, Luke's best has not proved to be good enough. I am sure that he never expected generations of scholars to spend their entire working lives dissecting the pages of his text line by line, word by word, letter by letter, squeezing every drop of meaning, weighing every expression. His narrative was never meant to bear such scrutiny: no wonder that the result has been centuries of debate and confusion. Scholars have tried to match up the start of the common era, AD 1, at the moment when Jesus was born with the reign of Herod the Great (Luke 1.5; Matthew 2.1). Herod the Great ruled as king from 37 to 4 BC. They have tried to harmonize this with the census taken during Quirinius's governorship, while Augustus was Emperor of Rome (Luke 2.1; Acts 5.37 – this census probably took place in AD 6). And of course there is the appearance of a miraculous guiding star to take into account too (not mentioned by Luke, but in Matthew 2.2, 2.9).

The precise historical details cannot be convincingly harmonized. But as a historian I would be much more suspicious about the historical truth of the Gospel stories of Jesus' birth if they were totally consistent. It is in the very nature of accounts

11

given by different witnesses to different audiences in different places at different times that there should be such variations. We only have to think of significant moments in our own life which, when we look back, reveal themselves to have been crucial turning points. At the time we had no idea how momentous they would turn out to be. We had no thought of amassing evidence to prove a chain of historical connection between the insignificant past and the meaningful present. More likely, people look back later in life and begin to perceive the moments and words which encouraged them to take a new turn, or showed them a fresh opportunity. Only Jesus' mother could have told others (surely Joseph and Jesus first among them) of that annunciation-moment; we don't know who told Luke, or whether he read an account written by someone else. In any case there is no window-dressing of the scene, no lengthy explanation of the where and when or even the why. The story has not been elaborated with corroborative details to try and convince us of its accuracy.

Luke described Mary as a 'virgin'. The Greek word can mean a young woman who has never been sexually active; or simply a young woman (i.e. with no reference to sexual activity or status). Because Gabriel tells her that the Holy Spirit will overshadow her, and because he tells her this in answer to her question about how she can have a child when she 'knows not a man' (this is *exactly* what the Greek says), it is plain that the manner of the conception is miraculous rather than resulting from the union of a man and woman in the normal course of nature. The virginal conception of Jesus is popularly, but misleadingly, referred to as the Virgin Birth. It is also sometimes confused with the Immaculate Conception, which is not directly about Jesus at all, but is the name given to a belief made binding on all Roman Catholics in 1854. This teaches that Mary was conceived 'without spot of sin' (the word 'immaculate' in Latin

means 'without any spot'). The identification of sexual intercourse with sin and taint is highly significant, and we shall
come back to it in Chapter 3, pp. 40–1; but it is no part of Luke's
understanding of Jesus' virginal conception. He has a higher
purpose. For him, the overshadowing by the Spirit evokes
the opening chapter of the book of Genesis ('the Spirit of God
was moving over the face of the water', 1.2), to imply that the
birth of Jesus will be a new beginning for the world. John does
something very similar at the start of his Gospel, when he uses
exactly the same opening words as those which begin the book
of Genesis ('In the beginning').

So Mary was a virgin when she conceived Jesus, who was
God's only-begotten son (John 1.14). We are left in no doubt,
as we read, that something unique is taking place. Much of the
later understanding of the meaning and person of Jesus was
built upon this miraculous conception: it came to be seen as an
ideal standard, of which all other conceptions are imperfect
copies, and so had far-reaching consequences for the Church's
attitude to sex both within and outside marriage. This is clearer
when we think about Matthew's version of the annunciation
(1.18–25), in which Joseph's first reaction to finding out that
his fiancée is pregnant is to disown her. He chooses, kindly, not
to expose what he regards as her shame; but the fact is, that
being a 'just' man or a 'righteous' man, he still decides to reject
her. His was a culture which prized and policed female chastity,
because that was the only way to ensure a posterity, through
children conceived within marriage. In modern Britain, much
of the stigma attached to pregnancy outside marriage has
disappeared (though in ethnic minority communities the issue
of 'honour' killing of women suspected of transgressing sexual
and moral boundaries is beginning to be taken seriously). Yet
marriage remains relatively popular. Still, the marriages which
are most likely to fail are those of teenagers from lower-income

backgrounds – exactly the situation in which Mary found herself. As a society, we need to find a way to face up to the consequences of widespread relationship breakdown, including a less stable home environment for many children, and all the complexities of stepfamilies. We also need to handle those consequences without judgemental attitudes, or crude 'one-size-fits-all' assumptions about what shape our social and family groups and networks ought to take. In this, as in so much else, Jesus, in his own human life, shows us the way forward.

In any case what Luke was trying to emphasize was not that conception without intercourse proved the moral purity of Mary or Jesus, or that chastity is superior to ordinary marriage (though these did emerge later as morals drawn from the conception of Jesus). Far from it. He was making the point that the Holy Spirit was interwoven in the very fabric of Jesus' being: the same Holy Spirit which is so central to his story of the Gospel and the birth of the Church. The same Holy Spirit which is God's gift to those he chooses for particular callings. Luke was also trying to show how the moment of the conception, rather than the birth itself, was the point at which the new creation began, that it was the moment when God entered into human history by taking on the experience of human finitude, in order to transform it.

So what is popularly referred to as the virgin birth should really be described as the virginal conception of Jesus. Those who doubt it as a scientific possibility can still appreciate the uniqueness of Jesus, and many people do. I myself once found it easy to dismiss the virginal conception as a historical fiction based on a misunderstanding of a Greek translation of the original Hebrew of Isaiah 7.14, where the word 'young woman' is taken to mean 'virgin'. That did not stop me worshipping as a Christian, or believing in Jesus as Lord. My beliefs may have been contradictory rather than logical – but that is where I found myself once. Not any more. The more I read and reflect, the more truth I discover in the annunciation story. This change in my understanding has come about partly through academic study of the Gospel texts, but also through my experience of the annunciation in prayer. In praying the joyful mysteries, I close my eyes and wait for an image of the scene to present itself to my mind's eye. I cannot see faces, but I do perceive figures, sometimes the young woman, at other times the angel. Mary may be at work in the temple, sweeping and polishing when Gabriel greets her. Sometimes she is at home, alone, sewing or sitting still. Sometimes I perceive nothing but a presence: light, voices, sometimes a rushing wind, darkness and sudden flashes of brilliance. Occasionally – very occasionally – the picture has moved from my meditations of mind and spirit into the core of my being. Then I do not so much feel that I behold what I meditate on, but rather know that I am part of it, and that it is part of me. It is because of this experience of the annunciation in my prayers, more than anything else, that I have come to believe in it so absolutely. I believe too, though, in the human right and duty to question, to ask about the meaning and morality of the events as they are told to us. These matters too become part of our praying of the joyful mysteries, because such prayer is not about escape from the world as we know it, but rather about encountering that world in order to transform it.

As we move through these mysteries, we are seeking historical, theological and spiritual truth. In the case of the annunciation, we have already seen how this can work – we are right to want to know what actually happened to Mary, and when and how (historical truth). We are right to seek after what it means for us today, and how we ought to set it in a wider context of God's plan for the world (theological truth). We are right to try and take it into our Christian identity, to pray it and live it (spiritual truth). This book is merely a starting point for the journey.

A prayer for the annunciation

God our Father,

Mary the mother of Jesus found the courage to say 'yes' to
    you.

Because I did not choose you, but you chose me,

help me to find the way through all the doubts and
    challenges I face,

so that I can bear fruit of your maturing,

and find the peace which only you can give,

in saying 'yes' to you;

through Jesus Christ our Lord. Amen.

Questions

1 Why did God choose Mary and not someone else?
2 Is it a good thing to challenge people's beliefs, or does that undermine faith?
3 Should we be worried by problems in the Gospel stories?
4 Was Joseph wrong to think of rejecting Mary?
5 How does imagining ourselves as part of the scene help our praying?

2

The visitation

Luke 1.39–56
In those days Mary arose and went with haste into the hill country, to a city of Judah, and she entered the house of Zechariah and greeted Elizabeth. And when Elizabeth heard the greeting of Mary, the babe leaped in her womb; and Elizabeth was filled with the Holy Spirit and she exclaimed with a loud cry, 'Blessed are you among women, and blessed is the fruit of your womb! And why is this granted me, that the mother of my Lord should come to me? For behold, when the voice of your greeting came to my ears, the babe in my womb leaped for joy. And blessed is she who believed that there would be a fulfilment of what was spoken to her from the Lord.' And Mary said, 'My soul magnifies the Lord, and my spirit rejoices in God my Saviour, for he has regarded the low estate of his handmaiden. For behold, henceforth all generations will call me blessed; for he who is mighty has done great things for me, and holy is his name. And his mercy is on those who fear him from generation to generation. He has shown strength with his arm, he has scattered the proud in the imagination of their hearts, he has put down the mighty from their thrones, and exalted those of low degree; he has filled the hungry with good things, and the rich he has sent empty away. He has helped his servant Israel, in remembrance of his mercy, as he spoke to our fathers, to Abraham and to his posterity for ever.' And Mary

remained with her about three months, and returned to her home.

When we looked at the first joyful mystery we considered how we can relate a story in Scripture to today's world. This is just as much of a challenge when we come to the second, the visitation. It is a scene of meeting. Two women who are pregnant greet each other in a moment of celebration. That meeting has theological significance: it teaches us about how people relate to God. It also has historical significance: it teaches us about how people relate to one another. The two kinds of meaning are interwoven – they point to the human need to *connect*, to depend both on one another, and upon God who is the source of all being and life. Much later, Luke takes this theme even further when he recounts Paul's declaration to the Athenians that God is intimately involved in the lives of all peoples and communities, not just the Jewish people. The days when each nation had its own god (or gods) have come to an end: '[God] is not far from each one of us, for "In him we live and move and have our being"; as even some of your poets have said, "For we are indeed his offspring"' (Acts 17.27–28).

In the communities to which Jesus and John were born people were looking for a *someone*, a *something*; but there was no agreement about what was to happen and how. These were days of expectation, as much for the people of Israel as for the two women whose hug has come to stand for that unique moment of disclosure, when the good news is first communicated.

To put this meeting in context, we must first move back to an earlier section of Luke's Gospel. The prayer of the joyful mysteries puts events in theological order, by starting with the annunciation. But Luke puts things in chronological order, and starts with the story of the Forerunner, John the Baptist. So the best way to understand the meeting between Elizabeth and

Mary is to look forward in time, to the relationship between their two remarkable, and sometimes difficult, sons.

We know all about Jesus (or we think we do). But who was John? He appears in all four Gospels as the person whose mission awakens Jesus' ministry. The relationship between them gives us some clues about how Jesus understood his own identity at the point when his public ministry began. All four Gospels identify John as the 'voice which cries in the desert', from Isaiah 40.3. Luke refers to the Isaiah prophecy in a passage immediately following the last of the joyful mysteries, the finding in the Temple (Luke 2.41–52):

> The word of God came to John the son of Zechariah in the wilderness; and he went into all the region about the Jordan, preaching a baptism of repentance for the forgiveness of sins. As it is written in the book of the words of Isaiah the prophet, 'The voice of one crying in the wilderness: Prepare the way of the Lord, make his paths straight.' (Luke 3.2–4)

For Luke, John is a *fulfilment* of God's promises declared by the mouth of the prophet. One of the many attractions of the Christian 'Way' for those first believers was that it offered authentic insight into the divine. Prophets were everywhere then, as now, predicting the future, and misleading the gullible. It was the same story in the Old Testament too – Isaiah warns against 'the astrologers, the stargazers, the monthly prognosticators' (47.13, AV). So the very fact of John's appearance as the voice in the wilderness, Luke thought, confirmed the identity of Jesus because it was a *fulfilment of prophecy*, and so a proof that God had pronounced on the matter of his identity.

Matthew also – following Mark – affirms this identification of John as 'the voice' (Matthew 3.3; Mark 1.1–3). Prophecy clusters around John: when he 'goes before the Lord to prepare his way' (Luke 1.76) according to the prophecy of Zechariah (1.68–79), there is another echo from the past (Isaiah 40.3; Malachi 3.1). For Luke at least, and probably for Jesus too, John's arrival was seen as heralding the 'day of the Lord' (Malachi 4.5). Judgement is drawing near.

Things are never as simple, though, as they first look. John is not only the 'voice': he is identified by the first Christians with Elijah, for there was widespread expectation at that time of Elijah's return, and John dressed, lived, spoke and behaved like Elijah. But John himself may have denied it (John 1.19–23; and see Acts 13.23–25). John could have claimed to be many things, but he does not. Instead, his words and actions show that anything which might detract from his message must be set aside. He claims just one function, one unique essence – to be the 'voice' spoken of by the prophet. Perhaps his father had sung the Benedictus not only at his birth but also during his infancy and growth to manhood. Perhaps that really was how he understood his dangerous and difficult calling. Perhaps for him, his whole life had but a single purpose – to be the 'voice'. If this is a picture of Christian vocation, it is terrifyingly austere.

There may be disagreement over details, but all four Gospels identify John as the 'voice in the desert'. Luke has no hesitation – John simply *is* a new Elijah. This is beyond doubt because the identification is not made by any fallible human being, but by the angel Gabriel who stands in the very presence of God (Luke 1.19). In his words to Zechariah foretelling John's future role, Gabriel says, 'he will go before him [Jesus] in the spirit and power of Elijah, to turn the hearts of the fathers to the children, and the disobedient to the wisdom of the just, to make ready for the Lord a people prepared.' Mark does things briefly, and differently (Mark 1.1–8). Matthew also has his own angle, recording how Jesus revealed the role of John in terms of the Kingdom:

Jesus began to speak to the crowds concerning John: 'What did you go out into the wilderness to behold? A reed shaken by the wind? Why then did you go out? To see a man clothed in soft raiment? Behold, those who wear soft raiment are in kings' houses. Why then did you go out? To see a prophet? Yes, I tell you, and more than a prophet. This is he of whom it is written, "Behold, I send my messenger before thy face, who shall prepare thy way before thee."

Truly, I say to you, among those born of women there has risen no one greater than John the Baptist; yet he who is least in the kingdom of heaven is greater than he. From the days of John the Baptist until now the kingdom of heaven has suffered violence, and men of violence take it by force. For all the prophets and the law prophesied until John; and if you are willing to accept it, he is Elijah who is to come. He who has ears to hear, let him hear.'   (11.7–15)

These differences of focus in how the evangelists understood John suggest that the identification of John with Elijah took time to emerge (see also Mark 9.11–13; Matthew 7.10–13).

Matthew sees John's suffering both as a reflection of the suffering of Elijah and as a forerunner of that of Jesus. He knows that in days gone by the prophets have suffered for proclaiming God's word; and John is nothing but his words, he is only 'the voice'. Christians in Matthew's day too were suffering for their faith, enduring martyrdom for the sake of the gospel. And John, the first to recognize the Lord for what he was (John 1.29), was also the first to die for the sake of the Lord and his Kingdom. Our God is certainly a God of surprises. He did all the hard work of creation to make a Paradise for Adam and Eve so that they could enjoy endless bliss. And yet he crowns those who do his will with thorns, with martyr crowns. So God reveals, through John the Baptist, the triumph of divine love – by a blessing which comes not by the granting of wealth or privilege, but through the grace of suffering and the glory of that martyr's crown.

John the Baptist is more than just the Forerunner who prepares the way for Jesus. His conception is miraculous: a lesser miracle, perhaps, than the virginal conception of Jesus, but a miracle nonetheless. It echoes a much older story – the story of Hannah and her son Samuel (1 Samuel 1—2), and with good reason: Luke uses the familiar story to make sense of the new story he urgently desires to make known. Hannah's miraculous child grows up to be a prophet, who anoints the first kings of Israel, Saul and David. Luke will reveal John the Baptist as a prophet who prepares the way for a new and infinitely greater king.

When we have read Luke's Gospel and the Acts of the Apostles together, it is obvious that the most distinctive theme of both, and what links them both together, is the working of the Holy Spirit. The Spirit is a force for change, inspiration and revelation in both people and events; a sign of the authenticity of the Kingdom which is being established. That theme began with the annunciation; it continues here. Gabriel promises Zechariah (and Elizabeth) a son, who will be called John, and will be filled with the Holy Spirit 'even from his mother's womb' (1.15). This same Holy Spirit is next declared to 'come upon' Mary (1.35) in the working of one of the greatest of all wondrous signs – the conceiving of a child by a woman who is still a virgin. Here is a spirit of prophecy and, unmistakeably, of the true divine presence and power.

The way in which this angelic promise is fulfilled marks John out before he is even born. He is uniquely gifted while still within his mother's womb – when Elizabeth heard Mary's voice, Luke tells us, the baby 'leaped in her womb; and Elizabeth was filled with the Holy Spirit'. For Luke, these two facts are inseparable; John is singled out as the one who recognizes and responds to the presence of the Lord (a title which marks Jesus' divinity, and which Luke gives 'to Jesus even during his lifetime) from the first moments of his existence. Just as with the obedience of Mary, so with the pregnancy of Elizabeth, we have learned down the centuries to process their reactions in spiritual terms; this can obscure the real extent of the demands God made on them, in a culture which had little tolerance towards women suspected of transgression of sexual norms (Mary) or who failed to produce legitimate offspring (Elizabeth).

The role of 'recognizer' or 'acknowledger' is confirmed in the Gospel of John the Evangelist, who states that the Baptist recognizes the presence of his Saviour by hailing Jesus as 'the Lamb of God who takes away the sin of the world' (John 1.29). This is crucial. The ability to recognize, to see truly and authentically what another person is, and what quality of meaning their life contains, is not only a Bible virtue, connected with those who see Jesus for what he is. It is the same quality which makes human relationships possible at all. Our families and friendship groups are knit together simply by this – one modern writer sums it up by saying that 'Love consists in recognising the needs of the individual'.* In meetings like the visitation, in family relationships and friendships, and in the Gospel: the ability to respond to God, to *recognize* the divine presence, turns out to be a quality not connected with effort, or right thinking. It doesn't really need words at all. First and foremost it is a gift *from* God; and following on from that, we discover that it is a gift which can communicate itself to others. No wonder Luke insists on describing the Holy Spirit in personal terms. The Holy Spirit is the indwelling *someone* who makes us capable of recognizing God, in other people, in ourselves, and ultimately in himself. Some modern theorists say that family breakdown in society is linked not to a failure to love – nothing

---

* Axel Honneth the sociologist and philosopher.

seems to have the power to eradicate our instinct to love! – but a failure to see other people with true insight (which only God can give). In other words, too often we fail to give proper *recognition* to the inner, most true, nature of others. People need to be recognized and accepted for what they truly are, rather than our faulty, partial images of them. The Holy Spirit, the Communicator between God and us, makes possible this recognition which leads us to the freedom of deepest divine love. We cannot love God at all unless we accept that such love can only be real when we have first learned to love one another – warts and all (1 John 4.20).

The Holy Spirit, so important to Luke, makes us ask *how* God is active in the world, and among us. When Elizabeth and Zechariah are 'filled with the Holy Spirit', they speak aloud, and speak words of truth (1.41, 67). At the moment when Mary arrives, Elizabeth cannot know that she is pregnant, so it is by the Holy Spirit's power that she recognizes and declares the fact – 'she exclaimed with a loud voice'. The same power of *knowledge* and *proclamation* enables Zechariah to prophesy. The Holy Spirit is the One who gives public voice to the secret things of God.

Where this extraordinary new theology comes from we do not really know. It seems likely that Luke reflected long; partly on his personal experience of salvation, partly on his observations of the effects of the gospel in others' lives, and partly also on what he had learned from the Old Testament. So finally, from all this, and doubtless from prayer and worship too, he forged a powerful new theology to fit the facts of his experience.

How well does Luke's new theology of the Holy Spirit fit the facts of *our* experience? I have to make a confession at this point. My own direct experiences of God are far from numerous. In fact I can still count them on the fingers of one hand. Let me be clear what I mean by this. I am not talking now about the sense of God's presence among people gathered in worship –

the peace, or conviction, or truth, which may come in such circumstances. This feeling of the Spirit's presence comes often. Nor am I talking about the sense of being filled with the Spirit which comes when standing up to preach or pray; nor even about the glancing, slantwise glimpses which articulate the moments of the day, in the kind words and unexpected smiles of others, in the satisfactions of a job well done and done for love of him, or in the transforming eye which looks on 'ordinary' things and finds instead things of beauty and deepest meaning. In granting such experiences, God is generous indeed to all who will open their eyes to behold his presence ever about us. No, I am talking here about the intense, trembling-into-prayer, bare-feet-on-holy-ground, ecstatic moments of beyond-doubt communion with what the poet R. S. Thomas has called 'that other being'.

Such experiences of the divine are not easy to talk about, nor should they be. They are given by God to those who need them, when they need them, to be reflected over and pondered at length, not gobbled up in a reckless greed for more, or spread abroad as though their only point was to confirm God's existence or teach God's nature. When such experiences are disclosed it should only be with caution, and to help others with words of comfort (in both the meanings of that word – *strength* and *consolation*). In conversations between Christians, it often emerges that such divine encounters have taken place, but those who undergo them find it impossible to express what they have encountered, or presumptuous even to try.

The best biblical descriptions of this experience of mystical encounter come, I think, in the book of the Exodus. Others may be able to think of different examples, but for me two stand out – Moses' meeting with God in the burning bush, when God tells Moses his name; and his encounter on Mount Horeb, which left his face shining so that none could look on it (Exodus 3.1—4.17; 33.17—34.35). In the first case, the burning bush, we have a description of the mystical encounter itself. In the second example, we see how its effect can be lasting, for the one who experiences it and for those whom it touches at one remove.

The first time God disclosed himself directly (from the bush), Moses was not ready. But later (on the mountain) he came prepared, knowing a little of the glory he was to behold. In a similar way, our encounters are not always recognized at first for what they truly are. Sometimes it is only with hindsight that we realize what has happened to us. It is common, and understandable, to try to repeat such an experience, but this is rarely possible, even when the attendant circumstances are replicated. So we have to carry on doing the ordinary things of life, the daily service of work and prayer and meals and sleep and leisure. And know that the next such time will take us by surprise as much as did the first.

In his remarkable book *The Idea of the Holy* Rudolf Otto tried to describe and make sense of such encounters. He prefaced his book with some lines of verse which have been translated from the German as:

> The shudder of awe is humankind's noblest emotion.
> No matter how the world around us gilds this feeling,
> To our core we're gripped by the immensity.
>
> Goethe, *Faust* II, Act I

These lines encapsulate his theme, the exploration of the ineffable *someone* of whom we sometimes become aware, yet who is beyond description. Otto used the term 'the numinous' from the Latin word *numen*, meaning divine presence or power. He took seriously our sense of the 'numinous' as something not generated from within, but encountered from outside ourselves, a mystical awe which 'invades the mind mightily in Christian worship with the words "Holy, holy, holy"'.*

---

* *Das Heilige* (1917, English translation 1923), p. 17.

We encounter God for ourselves in rare but blessed experiences of the numinous and mystical. Such experiences cannot be expressed or contained verbally – yet this conflicts with our ingrained respect for words as conveyors of significance and meaning. If something matters to us, one of our first reactions is to turn to words to capture it, to immobilize the fleeting moment (in much the same way as, much more recently, we have learned to do by taking photographs). We are trained by the guidance of parents, teachers and clergy, to process our religious experiences in verbal terms. It is the most natural thing imaginable to feel the need to describe and explain them. It is also essential, if they are ever to be transmitted from one generation to the next, as the evangelists must have realized. But there is a wide gap between those primary experiences and our secondary records of them (such as descriptions, memories, photographs – and Gospels). This gap is something people are often not very aware of, not least because we are often so quick mentally to process the unfamiliar in terms of what *is* familiar, to restore the equilibrium of the safely comfortable and known.

When we try to describe religious experiences, we have to admit how inadequate our powers of description really are. Preachers are extra-sensitive to this problem, because they have a *duty* to communicate a sense of the divine, so they come up against the difficulty, week by week, of describing the indescribable. Our indescribable experiences, those word-inadequate moments of utter clarity of vision, of overwhelming certainty and blissful peace, are what draw us into church, impel us to worship, to seek interpretation of those experiences, and ways to repeat them. We go looking, that we may find. But when we get to church and discover that it is wordy and word-centred, the sense of disappointment can be overwhelming. The Word was made flesh in the person of Jesus of Nazareth; and ever since then, as the saying goes, Christians have been busily turning him back into words again. There really is more to God than words and definitions.

Through John the Baptist Luke has shown us a glimpse of God's plan, and how we can forward it by learning to accord genuine *recognition* to those around us. Only the Holy Spirit can make this possible. John's family has, for Luke, a theological and a historical purpose – to reveal the meaning of the infant Jesus. The babe leaping in Elizabeth's womb attracted the attention of theologians in the early Church. They interpreted this action of the Holy Spirit as marking John out to be unique. Because they believed that the presence of the Holy Spirit was incompatible with sin, they thought that John must have been made holy while in the womb. The same line of thought was to lead to the belief that Mary was free from sin, for how else could she have been worthy to conceive the Saviour? or to encircle his growing body with her own mortal flesh? So it is not surprising that both were honoured from early times.

Even the Christian calendar highlights this understanding of how John first points to Jesus, and then makes way for him. It sets the birth-celebrations for John and Jesus (six months apart, Luke 1.36) on what were originally the lightest and darkest days of the year. John's birth is marked at midsummer, after which the light decreases, as John himself decreases in importance. Jesus' birth is celebrated at midwinter, after which the light, like the Saviour, begins to grow stronger and brighter day by day (John 3.30).

The mystery of the annunciation started with one woman called Mary. The mystery of the visitation also starts with a woman, and discloses a little more of God's plan. By according true recognition to Jesus, Elizabeth and her unborn son show us a pattern for family living. Our society once had a clear blueprint for what a family should be, but now that such certainties have vanished, there is still a pattern to be seen in all lasting relationships; their strength does not depend on structures (hierarchy) or components (father, mother, 2.4 children) but on *attitude* – an attitude of respect which accords due *recognition* to each person. When families falter and friendships crumble, it is not because we cannot love, but because true love requires more than the fulfilment of our own wishes and longings. St Paul understood what was right for his life, but still could not make it real; many parents discover the same truth. They want to do what they know to be right for their children, yet their own unrecognized needs get in the way of their instinct for goodness. To understand, and be understood completely is the goal for which we strive (1 Corinthians 13.12).

Like a jewelled miniature, the visitation encapsulates our mystical experiences. Ordinary things happen, but extraordinary things emerge from them. This culminates in the natural human desire to turn mystical encounter into words, and vision into prophecy ('My soul magnifies the Lord', 1.46: like her son, Mary seems not to fear the adverse judgements of other people, despite her scandalous pregnancy). If the emphasis in the first mystery was wonder, here it is joy, for here the Holy Spirit is introduced as the enabler of prophetic utterance and discloser of God's plan (1.42–43). It is not yet clear to either woman, or to those reading Luke's Gospel for the first time, what being 'Son' and 'Lord' will entail for Jesus. Luke's job is to unfold this, and much of it is dark and sorrowful stuff – salvation comes only through the passion of Jesus (Acts 2.36). The story begins, however, with joy, which is a truer reflection on the salvation story as a whole: Elizabeth exclaims to Mary, 'Blessed are you among women, and blessed is the fruit of your womb.' As we found already, being called 'blessed' in this new dispensation might mean something very different from usual expectations of blessing (wealth, security, long life, comfort). Yet the one who calls is faithful (1 Thessalonians 5.24); and we need to learn to trust him when he does.

A prayer for the visitation

God our Father,
you fill me with your Spirit,
and inspire me with your love:
Give me the courage to let go of self,
and so become more open to your infinite possibilities,
through Jesus Christ our Lord. Amen.

Questions

1 Is the life of John the Baptist just a means to God's ends?
2 What are the signs of the Holy Spirit at work in people?
3 Is it ever possible to put mystical experiences of God into
   words?
4 Does it matter whether Jesus was born on 25 December?
5 Do you think you truly recognize God in your closest family
   members and friends? In the stranger you meet on the bus
   or in the homeless man or woman on the street?

3

The nativity

———◆•◆•◆———

Luke 2.1–21

In those days a decree went out from Caesar Augustus that all the world should be enrolled. This was the first enrolment, when Quirinius was governor of Syria. And all went to be enrolled, each to his own city. And Joseph also went up from Galilee, from the city of Nazareth, to Judea, to the city of David, which is called Bethlehem, because he was of the house and lineage of David, to be enrolled with Mary, his betrothed, who was with child. And while they were there, the time came for her to be delivered. And she gave birth to her first-born son and wrapped him in swaddling cloths, and laid him in a manger, because there was no place for them in the inn. And in that region there were shepherds out in the field, keeping watch over their flock by night. And an angel of the Lord appeared to them, and the glory of the Lord shone around them, and they were filled with fear. And the angel said to them, 'Be not afraid; for behold, I bring you good news of a great joy which will come to all the people; for to you is born this day in the city of David a Saviour, who is Christ the Lord. And this will be a sign for you: you will find a babe wrapped in swaddling cloths and lying in a manger.' And suddenly there was with the angel a multitude of the heavenly host praising God and saying, 'Glory to God in the highest, and on earth peace among men with whom he is pleased!'

When the angels went away from them into heaven, the shepherds said to one another, 'Let us go over to Bethlehem and see this thing that has happened, which the Lord has made known to us.' And they went with haste, and found Mary and Joseph, and the babe lying in a manger. And when they saw it they made known the saying which had been told them concerning this child; and all who heard it wondered at what the shepherds told them. But Mary kept all these things, pondering them in her heart. And the shepherds returned, glorifying and praising God for all they had heard and seen, as it had been told them. And at the end of eight days, when he was circumcised, he was called Jesus, the name given by the angel before he was conceived in the womb.

The annunciation and visitation challenge us to make connections between Bible stories and real life. When it comes to the nativity, Luke has done the work already – he is at least as interested as we are in the truth of what happened. He doesn't turn to proof texts from Scripture in his story of the birth of Jesus. But then we would not expect him to, as he was writing for foreigners, for whom these texts had not the same authority and sanctity as they did for Jews. He doesn't claim that the nativity was a fulfilment of prophecy. This is in contrast to Matthew, who works much more as we might if we were writing a history of Jesus' birth, by seeking *corroboration*. He writes for Jewish readers. He has searched their Scriptures for texts to explain the meaning of the life of Jesus. He has found the answer in prophecies of the Messiah (Isaiah 42.1–4; Matthew 12.17), of the suffering servant who was to bring healing for the sick (Matthew 8.14). Having found in Scripture the answers and explanations he needed, he expects the testimony of those Scriptures to be persuasive for his readers.

Luke's Gospel nativity story communicates the meaning of Jesus' birth so brilliantly to us precisely because he does not rely on proofs from texts which non-believers have no reason to respect. So how does Luke invite readers in, and encourage them to pay attention to this amazing story? This question is more difficult than it looks, because we are accustomed to reading the Bible as if it were written for *us*, for *now*. If we want to answer it properly, we have to think about the people Luke was writing for in his own day. He surely did not imagine, as he set to work, how we would be studying and praying and singing his words centuries later. His first readers were probably people who heard Paul preaching the gospel message round the Mediterranean; or who 'caught' Christianity from their friends and neighbours. They heard the news of Christ crucified and risen, and they were hungry to know more, to devour every detail which could build them up in faith. Luke fulfilled that need. He gave them a picture which included more than just the miracles, more than the saving death and the mysterious empty tomb, more even than the risen Lord promising an outpouring of the Holy Spirit who was – and still is – the marker of authentic, transformative, joyful Christianity (Acts 1.8). He gave them a story which brought the Saviour and Lord closer to them than they could have thought possible. Luke showed them how their Lord, 'this Jesus', was truly like themselves, how their human frailty and mortality could be regarded as blessed by God, and not something to be despised. No wonder the nativity story is so revered.

Revered it may be; but it is not straightforward. Luke wrote for one group of Christians, Matthew for another. Different audiences, different priorities, different cultures. No wonder there are discrepancies between the two accounts. Matthew had cited Isaiah's prophecy that 'a virgin shall conceive and bear a son' (Isaiah 7.14 = Matthew 1.23, AV), but the original text of Isaiah did not refer to a virgin but a young girl (as noted above, p. 12). Luke said nothing about the birth being the fulfilment of Isaiah's prophecy. Does this mean that Matthew took the words of Isaiah in Greek and deliberately misrepresented them, fabricating a miracle birth to trump all other miracle births in the history of the Jewish people? Can we actually imagine him doing so? Add in the fact that Luke tells the same story from a different angle, and (as the most sceptical scholars would agree) using different sources; and it becomes harder and harder to see how such a story could have been fabricated so early on (within about fifty years of Jesus' death, and with plenty of people around who knew and remembered his family). True, the infancy narratives of Matthew and Luke are not seamlessly integrated into the rest of their Gospels, both of which are occupied with the last few years of Jesus' life. For their opening chapters, though, it is clear that they both drew on stories which were circulating among Jewish Christians at an early stage in the development of the Gospels as we now know them.

None of this, however, can prove or disprove what happened to Mary, or how the birth took place. Just as with the empty tomb, we have no record of how the event unfolded or what it looked like. All we are told is that 'she brought forth her first-born son'. Our own experience shows that with even the most remarkable events in life – milestones and direction-changing commitments, relationships, jobs, marriages, children – memories become fuzzy at the edges over time. We recall some details more vividly than others, perhaps what the weather was like, or what we were wearing, or what we had to eat, or particular words and phrases which branded themselves on our memory, taking on an intensity of meaning. Yet if some details are to stay in focus, others must, by definition, remain blurred. We cannot focus on all details of any picture at the same moment. So also, in the case of the nativity of Jesus, many facts about the manner of his birth, and its meaning, remain opaque and blurred. Who, after all, was there to tell the tale? Only Mary. Perhaps there was a midwife too. It is more likely than not (given the cultural context) that other women were present at the birth, but no men. If matters followed a traditional course, Joseph would not have been present, though doubtless he would have waited nearby.

It is up to us to decide whether or not we are prepared to put our trust in the Gospel writers, and the traditions they drew on, and the Christians whose memories and records brought our faith into its current form. In the end, it is always a matter of trustworthiness and reliability. In every field of knowledge, not just Bible studies, we proceed by building upon the discoveries and experiments of past generations. We weigh the evidence as best we can, but in no field of knowledge is it possible to begin every inquiry from scratch. Some facts have to be assumed or trusted if progress in understanding is to be achieved. In the case of the Gospel infancy stories, inquiring into truth and reliability is especially sensitive. What damage might be done by a wrong conclusion? Who might be led astray or lost to faith by a biased interpretation of the evidence? Some readers will be unconcerned at what others detect as problems in the Gospels as they stand; but for many Christians the best course will be to distinguish between the solid core message of the nativity, and the problems of detail which may (but should not) undermine confidence in the overall reliability of the Gospel.

If we reject the idea of Matthew and Luke 'making things up' to emphasize the importance of Jesus – and however flexible ancient writers were with the arrangement of facts and events, and their embellishment, they did understand the difference between 'what happened' and 'what did not happen' – we are left with the possibility that their sources fabricated 'facts' which deceived the evangelists, or (and this is much the simplest explanation) that the considerable degree of concord between their versions speaks of a miraculous series of events, the details of which were not remembered with complete accuracy. The discrepancies and differences of focus arose principally because what mattered was the reality of Jesus' humanity, and the fact of his identity as God's Son, more than the secondary matters like shepherds and magi and stars. People remembered the meaning for themselves more than they remembered the facts for history. It is rather like the build-up to a marriage: before the wedding day, the details of dress and bouquet, cake and orders of service seem all-important. But afterwards, as memories blur, it is the *meaning* of the day which comes into sharp focus, and the true power of the vows (for only living them can make them real) comes to be understood.

This way of seeing things will not convince those predisposed to doubt, especially not those who see in the virginal conception of Jesus the root of Christian hang-ups about sex as being something evil. Some early Christian groups took the simpler view that Jesus was the son of Joseph as well as Mary (Matthew 1.16). Their views did not prevail against the majority who had identified, correctly, the significance of the whole nativity story as pointing to the true identity of Jesus. Some later Christian thinkers seized on the nativity story as a reason for arguing that abstaining from sex was a higher way of living than marriage and family life. Yet their views were instantly challenged by the majority of the Church's teachers, including Augustine, who is usually blamed for negative Christian attitudes to sex. This is because of his teaching about original sin (that sexual intercourse is the means by which the sin of Adam is, like an incurable infection, passed from one generation to the next). Christians who look to the miraculous nativity of Jesus as a foundation of their faith should take heart that there is good reason not to reject the traditional understanding of what happened. They should not allow an unintended consequence of that miraculous nativity (an anti-sex agenda) to be 'read back' into the story itself. The sensitivities of some Christians concerning contraception and abortion may ultimately be rooted in the miraculous conception. Certainly it is a sobering thought that human intervention could have prevented the incarnation, or cut it short. The vulnerability which God accepts in Christ is seen at its most shocking here. But the story is really a sign of the divine breaking into the human realm, not God proving that sex is bad and he wants us to have nothing to do with it, or that human 'interference' in the biology of birth is inherently wicked. Luke is trying to show us that the birth of Jesus has meaning for all of us.

The core truth stands solid and unshaken. But there is no point trying to deny that Luke's account of the nativity includes details which don't add up. There are problems with the historical accuracy of the journey to Bethlehem; however one tries to integrate the chronologies of the many characters mentioned in the story – Herod, Quirinius, Emperor Augustus, and the rest – the timing is askew. To take the most scientifically problematic of the details, the star: the association of the star with the magi's journey to Bethlehem may have its origins in a prophecy made by Balaam (Numbers 24.17): 'I see him, but not now; I behold him, but not nigh: a star shall come forth out of Jacob, and a sceptre shall rise out of Israel.' The prophecy is centred on the triumph of God's people, the star signifying divine favour and the sceptre marking royal status. In the ancient world, telling the story of a star in connection with the birth of some important personage was a way of underlining the person's significance, giving them an aura of divinity, or at least divine favour. Obviously no one back then had technical equipment for recording or verifying such events once they had happened. And it is impossible to tell at a birth which babies will grow up to rule or conquer the world, and which will one day damage or defile it. The movement of the star is Matthew's sign to the reader that the coming of Jesus was part of God's heavenly plan for humankind as prophesied by Balaam centuries before. Now the magi, Balaam's successors, had seen that the moment was at hand for the prophesied king to be born: the star is there to teach us the truth, but it is a theological truth, not an astronomical one. It is the same kind of truth as the Church has preserved by setting the nativity on the darkest day of the year, to stand for light shining in darkness, which the darkness has not overcome. The fact that we find belief in the historical truth of the star hard, but do not struggle so much with the theological meaning of the incarnation may be encouraging, if we are learning at last to see the signs of God at work in the small miracles of life as much as in mighty signs and wonders confounding what we think of as the laws of nature.

As far as the nativity itself is concerned, Mary and Joseph must go to Bethlehem for the birth, to underline Jesus' messianic status as one who belongs in the Davidic city. Yet the census is not only at the wrong time, it also cannot explain why Mary travelled with him, especially not when she was about to give birth, as only her husband's name would have mattered for census purposes. Women were virtually the equivalent of property, so did not count as citizens. The birth itself took place either somewhere where animals were kept (because of the manger, Luke 2.7); or perhaps it may have been a house (Matthew 2.11) or, according to a very different tradition, a cave. Some scholars point to texts from Isaiah (1.3, 'The ox knows its owner, and the ass its master's crib; but Israel does not know, my people does not understand') and Wisdom (7.4–5, 'I was nursed with care in swaddling cloths. For no king has had a different beginning of existence; there is for all mankind one entrance into life, and a common departure') to suggest that Luke is, like Matthew, showing how the events of the birth were fulfilments of Scripture.

So the question comes back simply to this: what do we believe actually happened? The problem with 'believing' the Gospel account is, as always, in those tricky conflicting details, for all of them – however small – have been accorded either historical, or theological, or spiritual significance, or all three. The theological meaning is unmistakeable: Bethlehem is the place of the birth, say Luke and Matthew, who use lists of ancestors to underline as firmly as possible that Jesus was of the house of David. Herod the Great was king, says Matthew, because he sees Jesus as, on one level, a second Moses: so Herod is standing in for Pharaoh of Egypt, the arch-persecutor of God's people. The shepherds are first to hear the good news, says Luke, because for Luke the focus of Jesus' whole life is on the needs of 'the poor'. The first to *recognize* Jesus as King are foreigners (the magi) in Matthew's Gospel (2.2). Historical meaning is a harder matter. If we use facts such as these in our prayers, if we draw conclusions from them about who is in receipt of God's favour, with whom he is well pleased, what meaning lies within the events narrated, we want to know the historical value (i.e. the truth) contained in them. Yet we have to accept that a search for certainty will fail. We cannot reach intellectual certainty on this matter. After all, even when events in our own time take place before our very eyes, we are often uncertain about matters of both fact and meaning. Our point of view is only ever a partial one. With events of two thousand years ago, we are not wrong or foolish to put our trust in the integrity of those who wrote the Good News from their own experience of its transforming joy.

Whenever I conduct a service of holy matrimony, I begin with the words, 'Hear these words of scripture which are *tested and true*: "God is love, and those who live in love live in God, and God lives in them" (1 John 4.16, CW).' It is this kind of truth that we look for in the Gospel infancy narrative – truth which is *tested*. In the ancient world, people were more inclined than we are to believe that something which was plausible and coherent must therefore be true. We are more suspicious than they were of detecting meaning behind life events – we are less likely to see life in terms of tidy beginnings, middles and ends, never mind important moral messages! Perhaps it is *our* problem that we have a difficulty with the Gospel infancy narratives, and not the problem of the texts at all, because we live in a sceptical, suspicious generation. We were not always so in the past, we will not necessarily remain so in the future. Though we have become much more sophisticated, and cynical, about the ability of the written word to contain truth, never mind 'the whole truth' or 'nothing but the truth', we are not necessarily closer to understanding how to live at peace with ourselves, or in harmony with our neighbours and our environment.

So how can we pray the joyful mystery of the nativity? Not by shying away from the troublesome details, but by focusing on them instead. They are recorded for a reason, and that reason is always the same – because they have something to communicate about the gospel, as real people in real historical time encountered it. One way to do this is to focus on the simplicity of the scene. Luke does not even hint at some of the ideas which must have been 'in the air' as he wrote, but later writings uncover a clutter of speculation: did Mary give birth painlessly (because people thought she was undoing the 'curse of Eve', Genesis 3.16)? Did she remain miraculously a virgin (in the sense that her hymen remained unbroken by the baby's passage through the birth canal, hence the custom of continuing to refer to her as the Blessed Virgin Mary)? He relates the fact of the nativity without any suspicious corroborative explanations. The absence of detail allows us great freedom in our prayers, space to let our imagination go free, to paint the scene in our mind's eye and enter into it.

If Christmas is getting close now as you read this, your mind is probably full of practical matters, like whether or not you have ordered the turkey, and when you will find time to buy those last few presents. It can be hard to find time and peace to set all this aside and pray the Christmas story instead. We need to find help, by drawing on the strength of our knowledge and memories. If birth is part of our life experience through becoming a parent, we can draw on that experience for meditation: the reality, the solid undeniable humanness of birth, interprets for us the incarnation in which we put our trust. We have to resist any temptation to separate the birth of Jesus into a higher, purer category, because to be human is to live with dirt and defilement, pain and mortality. We cannot protect Jesus from all that, and we should not want to, because he chose not to remain apart from it, and instead accepted it willingly for our sake (Philippians 2.6–7). If birth is not something in which we have consciously participated, we can explore the nativity story through the way in which we know ourselves to have been born – coming into the world in a way of which we have no memory but the second-hand, fragmentary, out-of-focus memories of other people. But still we know it happened, and here we are. What we were once ('little, weak and helpless') and what we are now: they seem a world apart – and yet they are not. The common factor is our humanity, whether we are tiny infants, totally un-self-aware; or young people, or more mature, or on the threshold of entry into the next stage of Christian existence.

So is the devil in the details? Quite the reverse! We want to know which of the details are true because this is the story in the Gospels which is most familiar, heard in earliest childhood, repeated and reflected upon. In this case the details matter to everyone. If we hear the nativity story at all, we are most likely to do so as part of a culture saturated with commercial images of Christmas as a time of indulgence in food, presents and idleness. So to pray it in a real way, our understanding has to find the goodness in people's real experience of Christmas – the genuine understanding of the blessing of community which underpins every school nativity play; the human yearning for love, for generosity, for time shared which brings people together to eat and drink and rest; the crying need for a sabbath rest from drivenness and the pointless pursuit of passing pleasures which draws people to church in their thousands, to witness light shining in darkness, and to find a better hope beyond our strivings for success.

How should we react to the commercial Christmas which swamps us from September on? It is so tempting to separate ourselves and insist on our way of celebrating as the only true and right one. We should stop this once and for all. Christians may not approve of the way non-Christians celebrate 'our' festival: but we are too prone to disapproving and judging others for our own good. True, the heart of the celebration belongs to us because we have heard the message of the incarnation and done our best to respond; but the outpouring of God's grace lights on all who bear his image and likeness (Titus 2.11; 1 Timothy 4.10). There are reflections of the Truth in everyone who joins in the Christmas celebration.

'And she gave birth to her first-born son and wrapped him in swaddling cloths, and laid him in a manger, because there was no place for them in the inn.' This is how the Word became flesh and dwelt among us – and we beheld his glory. Glory? What kind of glory is this? Surely not the kind we expected! We ought to feel shock at the *ordinariness* of this birth. The first joyful mystery was indeed miraculous (in the sense of being contrary to nature), but the 'only' miracle in this mystery is the same miracle we ourselves were part of when we were born into the world; and it is none the less a thing of wonder for all that. So when we look deeper, by meditating, by praying ourselves into the scene and becoming part of it – in the birth of Jesus we behold an icon of ourselves. For some of us, the poverty of our surroundings will be material, like his; for others, that poverty will be spiritual. For all of us, there will be the same helpless vulnerability and hunger; the same need for motherly love; for the care and support of other people, on whom we have to learn to depend, whom we must begin to trust, if our physical and spiritual selves are to develop and mature. In this moment not only a baby but a family too is born – a sign both of our *need* for others and our *responsibilities* for others. As yet, we readers of the Gospel are still fly-on-the-wall beholders of an intensely private moment such as few are privileged to share. But though life may begin in privacy, it cannot remain there. Even here the infant is witnessed by the shepherds; and he is marked by the sign of the covenant as one of the people of Israel, so coming under the Law. His name, as Gabriel foretold, is Jesus, which means both 'God saves' and 'God, help!'. In those two meanings of his name, a statement and a prayer, there is a double image of our faith and hope. In the simple fact of his existence is the greatest promise – of God's love.

A prayer for the nativity

God our Father,
your Son's birth is a human icon
of your divine love for me,
and for all your children:
guide me in my daily living
to behold the truth of the incarnation,
and so turn my spiritual poverty
into the full riches of the Gospel promise,
through Jesus Christ our Lord. Amen.

Questions

1 How does Luke encourage us to hear his story?
2 How can we imagine the birth of Jesus, and what does our own life experience contribute to this?
3 Should the Church make people feel guilty about having fun at Christmas?
4 If Jesus was born of a virgin, can he really be fully human, like us?
5 What details of the nativity story are most important to you in your thoughts and prayers, and why?

4

The presentation in the Temple

———◆———

Luke 2.22–40

When the time came for their purification according to the
law of Moses, they brought him up to Jerusalem to present
him to the Lord (as it is written in the law of the Lord, 'Every
male that opens the womb shall be called holy to the Lord')
and to offer a sacrifice according to what is said in the law of
the Lord, 'a pair of turtledoves, or two young pigeons'. Now
there was a man in Jerusalem, whose name was Simeon, and
this man was righteous and devout, looking for the consolation of Israel, and the Holy Spirit was upon him. And it had
been revealed to him by the Holy Spirit that he should not
see death before he had seen the Lord's Christ. And inspired
by the Spirit he came into the temple; and when the parents
brought in the child Jesus, to do for him according to the
custom of the law, he took him up in his arms and blessed
God and said, 'Lord, now lettest thou thy servant depart in
peace, according to thy word; for mine eyes have seen thy
salvation which thou hast prepared in the presence of all
peoples, a light for revelation to the Gentiles, and for glory
to thy people Israel.' And his father and his mother marvelled
at what was said about him; and Simeon blessed them and
said to Mary his mother, 'Behold, this child is set for the fall
and rising of many in Israel, and for a sign that is spoken
against (and a sword will pierce through your own soul
also), that thoughts out of many hearts may be revealed.'

And there was a prophetess, Anna, the daughter of Phanuel, of the tribe of Asher; she was of a great age, having lived with her husband seven years from her virginity, and as a widow till she was eighty-four. She did not depart from the temple, worshipping with fasting and prayer night and day. And coming up at that very hour she gave thanks to God, and spoke of him to all who were looking for the redemption of Jerusalem.

And when they had performed everything according to the law of the Lord, they returned into Galilee, to their own city, Nazareth. And the child grew and became strong, filled with wisdom; and the favour of God was upon him.

In the first three joyful mysteries, we have been dealing with difficult historical and theological problems. What trust can we put in the Gospel texts? What are they really trying to communicate to us? Out of all these questions a pattern has begun to emerge. There is a distinctive progression in the joyful mysteries, the development of a spiritual matrix as it were, which reflects the real-life pattern of our encounters with God. It is always difficult to generalize about spiritual experiences, of course; and misguided to insist on one pattern as 'correct' to the exclusion of others. But where spiritual growth is concerned, what begins with the personal and individual cannot end there. If we are to grow in our spiritual lives, our experience of God has to be shared, and used.

What is this 'spiritual matrix', this pattern discernible behind the variety and details of our life in search of God? For most of us, it probably starts with moments of encounter, of awareness, of *presence*, for which we are quite unprepared. Even if we have been searching for a long time, such encounters still come as a surprise. Joy catches us unawares, and the journey commences. This first, individual, stage of the journey, in which our encounter with God begins, is reflected in the joyful mysteries by the annunciation story, with its divine message uniquely targeted for one unique person. The word is uttered, and heard, one-to-one, in that ultimate bare duality of the self and God. The angel speaks God's words on God's behalf. When the messenger from God speaks to *us*, we, like Mary, are called to respond – whenever, and however, those words come to us; and whoever is chosen to be God's angel speaking to us. God's choice of messenger is often surprising to us, and unexpected.

So the encounter between the divine and human begins, the spiritual matrix begins to take shape. Next, comes the dimension of communication from one human being to the next: the vision of God granted to an individual person has to be communicated to someone else. And I do mean '*has* to be communicated'. A genuine encounter with the divine presence *drives us* to go out and tell the good news, as Mary did: 'My soul magnifies the Lord.' The supreme example of this in Scripture comes from the prophet Isaiah, whose vision of God in his glory comes out of nowhere – 'In the year that King Uzziah died, I saw the Lord.' That is a moment of recognition, both of the Lord's holiness and of the prophet's own unworthiness; but also a challenge, to *do something*: 'Go, and speak to this people!' (Isaiah 6.1–9). The same spiritual matrix, of vision → recognition → communication (what we might call mission) is repeated again and again in Scripture and in human history.

In the visitation we found a meeting between those with open minds and grateful hearts, in which good news is communicated and so discovered to be a shared phenomenon, something in which the joy of one person can become joy for more than one. When it comes to the spiritual pattern of our own lives, we find that when we communicate our experiences of the divine to others, and find them to be shared, they become more, not less, precious and meaningful as a result.

The third stage in the revealing of this spiritual matrix is the progression towards a distillation of insubstantial words and hopes, promises and visions, into something tangible. In the joyful mysteries this 'something' is the nativity. Here, at the still centre of the joyful mysteries, is unfolded the heart of the Christian faith – that our salvation is not brought about by God rescuing our spirits from their prisons of flesh, but by the hallowing and transforming of that flesh, in other words our *bodies* as well as *souls*. Birth is the supreme physical reality which every human being experiences alike, however grand the circumstances or, as in the case of Jesus, however humble. To be divided from the one flesh we once shared with our mother, emerging into the light, the world, as distinct persons is a great as well as commonplace miracle. It is a moment, for parents and child, for Mary, Joseph and Jesus, as it is for every human being, when perspectives shift, and love has a chance to grow through the interchange of dependence and nurture. In the early days of Christianity, many thinkers who were attracted by the claims and stories of the new religion were nonetheless repelled by its insistence on what it called 'the flesh' (our earthly, physical bodies: see Genesis 3.19 and 1 Corinthians 15.35). It fell to the first great Christian theologian, Irenaeus, to defend it:

> I have given many proofs that the actual incarnate Word of God was hung on a tree; and even heretics admit that he was crucified.
>
> Clearly the Lord was coming to his own [John 1.10] and his own (which usually ought to be supported *by* him) came instead to be supporting him. Also, by his act of obedience on a tree, he brought about a repeat and reversal of that act of disobedience concerning a tree. Thus he undid that deception by which the virgin Eve (who was destined for a husband) was deceived; while the Virgin Mary (betrothed to a man) in truth received good news from the angel.
>
> (*Against Heresies* 5.18.1, 19.1)

So perhaps it is not surprising that, as he sees his own death drawing near, Jesus reflects upon this central mystery of human existence:

When a woman is in travail she has sorrow, because her hour has come; but when she is delivered of the child, she no longer remembers the anguish, for joy that a child is born into the world. So you have sorrow now, but I will see you again and your hearts will rejoice, and no one will take your joy from you.

(John 16.21–22)

He calls his mother to mind as he tries to prepare his followers for what is to befall him; soon afterwards, on the cross, he commends her to the care of the beloved disciple (John 19.26–27). The nativity is the pivotal event in the joyful mysteries because it bestrides the threshold between two worlds. It took place within the house (or stable? or cave?) away from public view, yet it was trumpeted by angels, celebrated abroad by shepherds. Until this moment, the joyful mysteries have been essentially private; but now a shift takes place, the shift from private to public life which every human being has to negotiate. We begin life in the dark cocooning of the womb, and then in the safety and privacy of a household and family. Yet the time must come when we have to emerge into a public world, to encounter strangers, form peer groups, and begin the long process of choosing, and paring away what will not form part of the pattern of our lives as our futures take definite shape. Babies, after all, are not meant to remain babies for ever. Part of the essence of our humanity is the inherent pattern of growth and development; and this means the closing down of some avenues as others open up.

The fourth joyful mystery, the presentation of Christ in the Temple, encapsulates this transition from the private sphere into public view and the communal world, reflecting the movement of the human soul in its progress in Christlikeness. We begin with private seeking and questioning, private turmoils, anxieties and hopes; but if we are to grow, our faith must become a matter of outward behaviour as well as inward conviction, a matter of doing as well as believing. The Church has

53

learned down the centuries that if faith is to develop, it must be celebrated in company with other people. One of the great strengths of the modern marriage service is the emphasis it places on the new life which a married couple begin together in the community. Practical and unromantic, this is not something which makes much immediate appeal as the words of the service are talked through with a couple before their wedding day. But it can takes on deep significance in later years.

Faith has to have a public as well as a private dimension. 'From all to whom much is given much will be expected' – there comes a time, as once there was of private exploration and solitary seeking, when we must return fourfold, with thanksgiving, in response to the joy with which Jesus receives us (Luke 19.1–10). Salvation costs us nothing, but our conscience tells us that our debt is incalculable. Just as we are driven to declare the wonderful gifts we have received, so too we are conscious that whatever we offer must be offered not grudgingly but joyfully:

> The point is this: he who sows sparingly will also reap sparingly, and he who sows bountifully will also reap bountifully. Each one must do as he has made up his mind, not reluctantly or under compulsion, for God loves a cheerful giver.
>
> (2 Corinthians 9.6–7)

In the 1980s, one of the most popular shows on TV was *Fame*, about a group of young people training at a New York City high school for the performing arts. In the opening titles, the dance teacher addressed her class with the words, 'You want fame? well, fame costs: and right here is where you start paying.' We could easily substitute the word 'faith' for 'fame'. There is a cost involved in public affirmation of faith, in the decision to live the Christian life to the full. It is a cost which cannot be repaid grudgingly, but only by service born from joy, as we begin to take up our place within the Church, becoming nurturers and builders-up of the next generation, as our predecessors were to us. This is what being the Church really means.

The presentation of Christ in the Temple is a family celebration to sanctify and make public the process of human birth. Jesus was born as we are, and his birth makes a difference to the fabric of the world, just as the birth of every baby does. Such changes require us to adjust, and to acknowledge the adjustment before God as a way of accepting the change into our individual and corporate lives. The birth of a child has a triple aspect: it causes ripples on the water of normality for the parents; also for the wider family and community; and thirdly for the infant itself. In this case, the birth is marked with respect to all three: Jesus is presented to the Lord as a first-born son; Mary is purified, and Simeon and Anna represent, by their reactions, the wider community of God's people. The song of Simeon, known as Nunc Dimittis after the Latin version of its opening words, interprets the events which we have been meditating upon thus far. He takes up the themes which we have been prepared for through the annunciation ('of his kingdom there will be no end') and visitation ('why is this granted me, that the mother of my Lord should come to me?'), responding to his first sight of the baby Jesus as the fulfilment of a divine promise. He then gives thanks to God for this blessing – 'mine eyes have seen thy salvation' (Luke 2.30). Here for the first time we learn for certain that the inclusion of all the nations is part of God's purpose in history – 'a light for revelation to the Gentiles and for glory to thy people Israel' (2.32; Isaiah 49.6).

Luke reveals the inclusion of the Gentiles in the divine promises as an indispensable part of God's plan. He treats the song of Simeon as a double fulfilment, both of an individual promise: 'It had been revealed to him by the Holy Spirit that he should not see death before he had seen the Lord's Christ' (2.26); and of a communal prophecy: 'I have given you as ... a light to the nations, to open the eyes that are blind' (Isaiah

42.6). Matthew takes a different path: he uses the journey of the non-Jewish magi, who come from far away in recognition of the divine message and who bear their costly gifts in recognition of divine kingship. In both cases, the message is one of inclusion. These two ways of pointing to the same message of inclusion of the Gentiles serve to corroborate a key element of the Kingdom he inaugurated. This corroboration surely ought to encourage us to trust its truth, not doubt it: the Kingdom of God is at hand: and *all* are welcome to enter into it.

Simeon does more than just sing. He also makes a sombre prediction, particularly directed at the mother of Jesus, in recognition that for her, as for all parents, future joy will be for ever bound up in the well-being of her child. Through Simeon, Luke foretells the grief that awaits Mary, who cannot, must not, turn her son from the path of suffering which he will choose. Even in the midst of celebration such seeds of sorrow are always present – Matthew points to the same truth through the magi's gift of myrrh, which was an ointment for embalming the dead. Human life can never be wholly insulated from pain; and joy, to be at its deepest, has to make room for this.

Jesus was born into a human family; and by his presentation in the Temple he was made part of a wider family – his people. When we are born we should not be alone, but should feel that we belong to parents, family, community, society. That is the ideal. Yet the reality can be dreadfully different. We are repeatedly shocked at discovering that parents can abuse and maltreat their children, and even kill them; and our shock is mingled with worry and guilt about the harm we may have inflicted in lesser ways ourselves. Have we hurt our little ones by our behaviour? Do we inflict on them our own anxieties? If it is difficult to accept that as parents we have a responsibility for harm suffered by our children, it can be as hard, or even harder, to face and admit the weaknesses of our parents. How reluctant children can be to admit that their parents have failed them or let them down! How desperately children try to cover up for their parents' unkindnesses, to defend them against criticism! The ideal of the family is still so strong, the pull of loyalty is so powerful, the dream of being loved unconditionally, and forgiven completely, is still so precious to us.

At Christmas, perhaps more than at any other time of year we feel the pressure to be happy, and the expectation that family harmony is not just desirable, but compulsory. This pressure in itself is often enough to trigger disputes and distress, as people come together to try and create a sense of togetherness for which they have had little or no practice during the rest of the year. The days are at their shortest, the weather at its coldest; and the temptation to venture outside at its lowest. Enforced proximity inside the house adds to the pressure. There are squabbles and arguments, relationships falter and break, domestic violence reaches the 'high' point of the year. Why are our good intentions so calamitously frustrated? And what can we do to set things right again?

The key to happiness at Christmas, or at any other family or community gathering, is to remember that perfection is an impossible dream; that, as one wise priest once said to me, ' "Good enough" really is good enough.' In our memories of childhood we tend to edit out the bad bits of Christmas, so that we remember only happy times. Whatever bad memories we cannot erase become woven in to our determination to do better ourselves in our own celebrations. So the pressure to achieve perfection increases. What is more, most of the impressions we absorb from our environment insist that such perfection is *achievable* – that we can bring about perfect contentment and perfect harmony in our family celebrations if we only try hard enough, and spend enough. Not even years of experience and the bitterness of repeated disappointment can deter us from striving for this goal. There is a dangerous side to the natural human desire for improving things – when it hardens into perfectionism, driven by that other dangerous human tendency, control-freakery, our own best instincts turn against us to our own destruction. We cannot make other people happy by our own efforts to control circumstances and reactions. We may succeed in purchasing temporary pleasures, but we can neither organize nor shop our way to joy. The pleasure that comes from arranging and buying things for people, real though it is, is but a counterfeit of the joy which comes by God's free gift to us. The question we face particularly at Christmas is how to secure the real, the lasting joy, without fooling ourselves with temporary substitutes.

The true answer to this puzzle is simple, and impossible to *make happen*. This is because it isn't about anything we do or don't do. Rather, it is about something that we can *be*, that we one day find that we are, that we have learned the hard way to become. The kind of self-understanding that comes after much reflection and prayer, and a degree of perception about ourselves and our needs and weakness, is our best hope for fulfilment within the context of the family or community. It is the only way to achieve the Christian virtue of patience, which really means an ability to endure not in grim determination but in sympathy and compassion for others. The foundation of happiness for families, as for individuals, is therefore not in money and property, not even in gifts (lovely though the act of giving can be): it is solidly and solely in allowing ourselves and others to be most truly ourselves, and taking joy from that act of allowing. And how hard, how very hard it is to become this!

In parish life, I began my ministry inspired by hopes of what I could do for those whom I was called to serve. Instead, I grew to become grateful for what they had taught and given me. In my present ministry the deepest joy comes from sharing in a search for the Truth. As with most clergy, my ministry has included a great deal of interaction with the elderly. But I could not have anticipated how much I had to learn from them. In saying this, I am not being sentimental – some elderly people are quite as selfish and self-centred as the young, equally hardened to the needs and claims of other people. Sometimes a life of isolation and loneliness, as mobility deteriorates and the circle of friends contracts, makes people more self-centred. Sometimes, though, it gives them a sense of perspective which I suspect (I am guessing here) comes to human beings by no other means than by the hard discipline of bodily weakness on the one hand, and sensitive reflection upon the human condition on the other. There is a chance of wisdom in old age which (again I cannot yet speak from experience but only from observation) is not self- but other-regarding: which looks on humanity, and the struggles of the young, and their unintended slights and heedless neglect, as God does; that is to say, with pity, not with blame.

The importance of all this is given a peculiar intensity by the presentation in the Temple. We encounter not only a family celebration of a religious observance, but within that an interaction of two extremely elderly characters with an infant barely more than a month old, a symbol of the circling years all the more poignant because this old age is something Jesus will not reach himself. Luke's words about Simeon suggest that he was very old; while there is no doubt that Anna, whom we would regard as elderly, was for those days extraordinarily aged. They both have gifts to offer the baby, as the magi did in Matthew's Gospel. Here the gifts are not objects but words inspired by the Holy Spirit. So the Holy Spirit is present at every turn in the narrative of Jesus' infancy. He inspires John the Baptist even in the womb; and he overshadows Mary. Then the Spirit triggers a series of recognitions, first within and then outside the family circle:

Elizabeth was filled with the Holy Spirit and she exclaimed with a loud cry, 'Blessed are you among women, and blessed is the fruit of your womb!' (1.41)

Zechariah was filled with the Holy Spirit, and prophesied, saying, 'Blessed be the Lord God of Israel.'   (1.67–68)

In the case of Simeon the recognition comes through inspiration so powerful that it triggers a triple reference to the Holy
Spirit:

> Now there was a man in Jerusalem, whose name was Simeon, . . .
> and the Holy Spirit was upon him. And it had been revealed to
> him by the Holy Spirit that he should not see death before he
> had seen the Lord's Christ. And inspired by the Spirit he came
> into the temple.   (2.25–27)

Thus the first manifestation of Jesus in the public sphere, before
he is capable of coherent speech, miraculous demonstration
or symbolic action, results in a double recognition. A man
and a woman, both devout Jews, recognize in the infant the
fulfilment of God's purposes. Luke shows the birth and childhood of Jesus as a time charged with awareness as if with a current of electricity, one recognition sparking off another. This
balances brilliantly the end of the Gospel, which is again charged
with significance, as Jesus is recognized for who he really is –
by the thief, the centurion, Cleopas and his companion at
Emmaus, and later by all the disciples (23.42, 47; 24.35, 36–43).

Often the Holy Family is taken as an icon of unity and harmony. This is the image we encounter here. Later in Jesus' life
the pattern changes, as he proclaims a radical discontinuity
between loyalty to family and loyalty to God:

> Then his mother and his brothers came to him, but they could
> not reach him for the crowd. And he was told, 'Your mother and
> your brothers are standing outside, desiring to see you.' But he
> said to them, 'My mother and my brothers are those who hear
> the word of God and do it.'   (Luke 8.19–21)

These words slice straight through the vision of Christianity
as a cosy family-orientated religion. They are directly symbolic

of the pull felt at some time by all Christians, between the demands of group loyalties (family, friends, workplace) and the imperative of obedience to God's commands. This is perhaps most intensely apparent in young adulthood. Then religion taught in childhood is either to be rejected as outmoded or deluded; or it is to be accepted but with open adult eyes, not with childhood loyalty. Loyalty to peers is not the same thing as devotion to the things of God, as we are about to find out.

A prayer for the presentation in the Temple

God our Father,
your love is for all your people, made in your image:
bless me with eyes to see as you see,
so that I may be what you call me to be,
and do all that I do, in silence or in speech,
with kindness and patience;
through Jesus Christ our Lord. Amen.

Questions

1 What does 'mission' mean to you?
2 Are we still surprised and disturbed by the thought that 'the flesh' matters?
3 Can you remember an experience of possible paths and futures closing down, or opening up, in your life? Did you feel the presence of the Holy Spirit guiding you?
4 Do you expect perfection from members of your church or from your minister?
5 Why are our spiritual good intentions not matched by results?

5

The finding in the Temple

---◆◆◆---

Luke 2.41–52
Now his parents went to Jerusalem every year at the feast of
the Passover. And when he was twelve years old, they went
up according to custom; and when the feast was ended,
as they were returning, the boy Jesus stayed behind in
Jerusalem. His parents did not know it, but supposing him
to be in the company they went a day's journey, and they
sought him among their kinsfolk and acquaintances; and
when they did not find him, they returned to Jerusalem,
seeking him. After three days they found him in the temple,
sitting among the teachers, listening to them and asking
them questions; and all who heard him were amazed at his
understanding and his answers. And when they saw him they
were astonished; and his mother said to him, 'Son, why have
you treated us so? Behold, your father and I have been looking for you anxiously.' And he said to them, 'How is it that
you sought me? Did you not know that I must be in my
Father's house?' And they did not understand the saying which
he spoke to them. And he went down with them and came to
Nazareth, and was obedient to them; and his mother kept all
these things in her heart. And Jesus increased in wisdom and
in stature, and in favour with God and man.

The last joyful mystery draws us onward to the adult life of
Jesus the man. It is ideal material for post-Christmas reflection

on the meaning of the incarnation, as thoughts turn to the beginning of Jesus' public ministry. The first thing we notice about the finding in the Temple is how odd it is. Unique, in fact. It is the only story in the whole of the Gospels which gives us any information about the boyhood of Jesus. If the other three evangelists did not decide to include such material, why did Luke think it was important? He recounts it as an historical report of an event in Jesus' life, but there is also a theological meaning to be uncovered. It bridges what Luke saw as a gap between the miraculous events surrounding Jesus' birth, and the start of his public ministry following his baptism by John (Luke 3.21). At the same time, it also bridges a different kind of gap, between a helpless baby Jesus unable to declare his own message and identity (the word 'infant' derives from a Latin word meaning 'unable to speak') and an adult Jesus proclaiming aloud the Kingdom of God.

This is the first time that the Word (to borrow a title from John's Gospel) is heard to utter a word: 'How is it that you sought me? Did you not know that I must be in my Father's house?' (Luke 2.49). The boy Jesus simply cannot grasp why his parents have misunderstood his intentions and actions – not so different from other adolescents, then. This double question of Jesus, in response to his mother's reproach, is very different from the first words of Jesus which Mark records. Jesus' first utterance reported by Mark is a public one, made as an adult; a challenge to all, not just to his parents: 'The time is fulfilled, and the kingdom of God is at hand; repent, and believe in the gospel' (1.15). These first words of Jesus immediately make the link with John the Baptist, 'a baptism of repentance for the forgiveness of sins' (Mark 1.4). They also tell the reader how John understood his own role, as a preparation for greater things, 'After me comes he who is mightier than I, the thong of whose sandals I am not worthy to stoop down and untie. I have baptized you with water; but he will baptize you with the Holy Spirit' (Mark 1.7–8). For Mark it is the *adult* Jesus, with his gospel message of the Kingdom, who matters. Though Jesus must have spoken countless words before this, this is the first time, for Mark, that his words matter, because this is the time of fulfilment. In Matthew too, the first recorded words of Jesus are of the highest significance: but in his case they are part of a conversation, and with a different theological purpose. Where Mark began with Jesus' proclamation of the Kingdom, Matthew begins with John the Baptist being reluctant to baptize Jesus (Matthew 3.11). When Jesus comes to be baptized, then, *John* looks for cleansing through baptism, but Jesus insists, 'Let it be so now; for thus it is fitting for us to fulfil all righteousness' (Matthew 3.13–15). As an entrance to the centre stage of world history, it is remarkably low-key; but it still conveys a powerful message about Jesus, especially his readiness to be 'done to' as well as to 'do', to receive from others as well as bestowing blessings. This readiness points forward to the passion, in which he becomes archetypally the one 'done to' instead of 'doing'. There is also deep significance in that phrase *for us*: Jesus begins as he means to go on, by including others in his mission, by speaking as one born *like us*, as *one of us*.

What about John's Gospel? He too has John the Baptist proclaim Jesus' identity before the Saviour himself speaks a word. He too, like Matthew, sets that proclamation within a context of challenge and opposition. He too records John's acknowledgement of Jesus' superiority. It is in this context that Jesus speaks for the first time in John's Gospel:

> The next day again John was standing with two of his disciples; and he looked at Jesus as he walked, and said, 'Behold, the Lamb of God!' The two disciples heard him say this, and they followed Jesus. Jesus turned, and saw them following, and said to them, 'What do you seek?' (John 1.35–38)

That question resonates down the centuries – 'What do you seek?' It demands a response. At the time, it must have made those who heard it ask searching questions about themselves. It is still the biggest question we can ask ourselves about the meaning of our lives. But are we brave enough to ask it? Are we wise enough to hear the answer? Are we strong enough to follow where it leads?

To look at the first recorded words of Jesus in each of the Gospels takes us into new territory. We are no longer asking historical questions (when and how did it happen?) but theological ones (what does it mean?), because we know that these words cannot be the first words Jesus ever spoke. Many Christians use the seven last words (or 'sayings') of Jesus on the cross for prayer and worship; there is no comparable tradition regarding the four first sayings of Jesus, yet they too are rich in meaning. There is no problem in interpreting them theologically (because we know for sure that they are words *chosen by the writer*). It would be possible to argue that the fact they are the first words spoken by Jesus in the Gospels is not significant; i.e. that Matthew, Mark, Luke or John did not think, when writing them down, 'This is the first time the Lord speaks in what I write.' But I think it is better to accept that these four sentences have profound importance for how we understand the gospel message as the evangelists wanted to record it. Among them, Luke's choice of words stands out distinctly:

Mark:	'The time is fulfilled, and the kingdom of God is at hand; repent, and believe in the gospel.'
Matthew:	'Let it be so now; for thus it is fitting for us to fulfil all righteousness.'
John:	'What do you seek?'
Luke:	'How is it that you sought me? Did you not know that I must be in my Father's house?'

Those Lucan first words sound straightforward enough. But they are not. For one thing, they are extremely difficult to translate. The Greek which Luke originally wrote doesn't include the word 'house'. It just says, 'Did you not know that I must be in *the* . . . of my Father'. The definite article, *the*, is plural, and stands for something else, but no one is sure what. The Authorized Version took the view that it means 'in the business or affairs of', and translated, 'wist ye not that I must be about my Father's *business*?' Later generations of Bible scholars argued it out and decided that, given the setting of the scene in the Temple, it probably referred to the building itself, 'in my Father's *house*'. It could even mean (at a push) 'among the *people* of my Father', referring to the teachers of the Law. Whichever of the three interpretations is correct, Jesus' questions set before the reader, in Luke's day and our own, the same contrast between earthly and heavenly, between blood family and spiritual family. The youthful Jesus takes for granted something which is completely incomprehensible to his parents: that the loyalties of blood family must be superseded by that higher loyalty which transcends all else – the call of God himself. Thus the theological message of those first words is multilayered. It confirms something about where Jesus belongs – 'surely it was obvious that I would be involved in *X*': whether it means the Temple, or some business, or the teachers of the Law, it is the same idea, of connection with the things of God. His advent, in other words, is a moment of conjoining with the adult world of religious observance, not a radical separation from it. That separation comes instead in the domestic sphere: family is going to take on a new meaning from this point on. Loyalty and faithfulness are due to the heavenly Father even before the earthly parents whom the Law commands every person to honour (Exodus 20.12).

What Luke is explaining here is the same insight that he highlighted by the nativity, as did Matthew (especially by prophetic fulfilment). And John led his readers even further back into the mysteries of God's purposes by stating boldly that 'in the beginning was the Word . . . and without him was not anything made'. All three insist, in their different ways, that Jesus was not selected by God at the moment of his baptism; but that from before the moment of creation (John) or at least from the moment of his conception (Luke, Matthew), Jesus was God's own Son. All three tease out, in different ways, what this meant for their readers. John's Jesus is wise to the point of omniscience. Though Luke and Matthew do not go this far, they still describe a Jesus who does and says things which reveal an understanding of God's will, and a consonance with his purposes, which set him apart from every other human being. This uniqueness makes their firm insistence on his being born as a human baby all the more remarkable (John alone gives full expression to the idea of his being incarnate, 'the Word was made flesh', 1.14). If we look closely at the text as Luke narrates it, we find that the point he is making is coherent with this insight into Jesus' true humanity. It may be that what we notice first (because we are conditioned to expect it) is a stress on Jesus' extraordinary wisdom. But the story is actually focused on something different. The 12-year-old youth, on the verge of manhood, does three crucial things:

1 he seeks out the wisest among his people;
2 he listens to what the teachers have to say;
3 he asks them questions.

This makes it plain that the conversation was not entirely one-way. Like all good teachers, those in the Temple that day were prepared to listen as well as to speak themselves – but then so was the young Jesus. He was prepared to listen and to learn. They were struck by his understanding and his answers, so they must have responded to his questioning by asking him questions in turn. It is an encouraging picture. It offers us hope that we can go deeper into the truth of God if we are able to avoid writing off the opinions and ideas of the young, and instead manage to pay attention to them. It is a two-way process, but with the emphasis on listening to the young – a counterpart to the previous joyful mystery, which the infant listened in silence as two elderly people spoke with the Spirit's authority about him.

The second element of Luke's message in the finding scene also uncovers something of Jesus' true identity, but there is no denying that it is problematic. Luke is undoubtedly making a point about *who Jesus truly is*. The words Jesus speaks to his reproachful mother make this obvious – 'did you not know that *I must be in my Father's house?*' (2.49). But we have to ask ourselves, Why? Why doesn't Mary seem to understand what he's doing there, when she has already had an angel telling her who her baby is, and how he will be conceived miraculously? We should also notice that Joseph is introduced as if he were simply Jesus' father, not his adoptive father. But then, by the time the story takes place, Joseph has stood in the role of father to Jesus for 12 years, ever since he was born – it is hardly surprising if Luke slips into describing him as a father when he has accepted that parental role for so long: not all 'real' fathers are 'blood' fathers. The proper contrast is drawn when Jesus himself distinguishes between his earthly father and his heavenly Father. We are not dependent on the virginal conception story of 1.26–38 for making sense of the teaching that Jesus was not of earthly paternal descent.

So there is a double message in this Temple scene: first, that Jesus, as a human being, had to *learn*, as we do, about the things of God. Second, there is the fact that his attitude to his human family was complicated. This contrast between the demands of an earthly and a heavenly family resounds in other Gospel passages (Mark 3.3; Matthew 12.46–50; Luke 8.19–21). If we find this awkward (one person told me that she thought Jesus came across, from reading the Gospels, as unacceptably rude to people!), it may be because we don't understand the finer nuances of the words. So for example when Jesus speaks to his mother by saying 'Woman, what have you to do with me?' (John 2.4), it may sound rude to us but it could have been a normal and usual form of address in that society and at that time. That may be true, but the fact remains that the basic message of the man Jesus in his words to members of his family is consistently a rejection of their appeals to his loyalty and obligation, in favour of a higher loyalty, to the things of God.

At 12, when he would have been on the verge of manhood as far as the customs of his people were concerned, Jesus rejects the claims of his parents that he owes them a regard for their anxiety, asserting instead that he is responding to another, presumably higher, claim on his regard and loyalty. His words to his mother at the time of the wedding in Cana point the same way. In a key moment in Mark's Gospel, almost at the beginning of his active ministry, his mother and brothers come to find him; 'they sent to him and called him', says Mark (3.31, see p. 60). Their call is reinforced by the words of the crowd which has gathered around him – perhaps because he had not responded to the first summons from Mary and his brothers, 'your mother and your brothers are outside asking for you' (3.32). His response is shocking indeed:

> He replied, 'Who are my mother and my brothers?' And looking around on those who sat about him, he said, 'Here are my mother and my brothers! Whoever does the will of God is my brother, and sister, and mother.'

This distinction between blood family and true family makes the finding in the Temple in one way the most awkward of the five joyful mysteries. This is partly because we have begun to encounter Jesus on the verge of adulthood; and as with anyone at that liminal moment, he has to negotiate that shift, and those around him have to accommodate themselves to his new role – it is not easy for either party. It is also because we must at last set aside the infant incapable of speech and action, and begin to deal with a reasoning, thinking, questioning, praying human being, whose independent adult personality will challenge us and make us reassess our priorities, our whole way of life. But like Adam and Eve in the garden of Eden, we have to grow up – human living is not going to be a refuge in Paradise. No blissful ignorance for us! Suffering and struggle have been our lot ever since the Fall (Genesis 3.16–19); but God will not leave us entirely unprotected (Genesis 3.21). Jesus shares this with us, as he shares everything else.

In times of human celebration, the joy which is ours is always interwoven with threads of sorrow, for the hopes of which we were disappointed, the plans which bore no fruit, the people we have loved but see no longer. The last joyful mystery points us forward into the sorrows which await Jesus in his adult life, as they await us all. By his incarnation he has entered into everything that we endure, even the growing pains of adolescence, and emergence into adult society. Somehow God works all our pain in together with the joys of life, as he does for Jesus. There is myrrh at the birth celebration, pointing forward to his burial; and a piercing sword for Mary, pointing forward to the suffering of all followers of the Son, all who take up the cross and walk in his footsteps – even his own mother.

The finding in the Temple is a story about *letting go*. For Mary and Joseph, it means accepting that their child is now growing up, and is 'his own person'. They have to learn to let go of the child and prepare to accept and respect the man. For Jesus, it is about learning to become that adult human being, not the property or shadow of his parents but a person in his own right – learning from others, and being listened to with respect himself. The spiritual matrix which has been gradually revealed in Luke's Gospel here reaches its completion. What began at an individual level, and moved through the stages of one-to-one communication, emergence into the world and engagement with community, is now fulfilled in the discovery of a double loyalty: both to community (in the domestic and public spheres) and, supremely, to God.

There are some people, a very few, who receive from God a call to live the solitary religious life. A true calling to such a life is exceptionally rare. Yet sadly too many people today are living the solitary life without either a call from God to make sense of such an existence, or a faith to sustain it. Instead they are trapped in a loneliness not of their own will or choosing. Unpractised in the arts of negotiation, compromise and tolerance which good community or family life should teach, they have no way of coping with the ties and claims of others. The upside of this is a high degree of personal freedom and autonomy. The shadow side of this independence is an inability either to experience or to appreciate how living as part of a larger, more diverse group can teach, confirm and nurture true maturity. There is little respect today for much that Christianity has to offer because its deepest insights are couched in language people no longer speak, or rely on texts which people no longer accord a special status. Yet the truth we should proclaim with confidence, rooted in the five sources of truth about God which we glanced at earlier (see p. x), is that Christian wisdom is rooted in real people's real experiences of God – and that the Scriptures are ancient witnesses to the living reality of our faith.

Real religious faith is the answer for those who live their lives in isolation, for whom society is a word without meaning; for whom community is a source only of demands and tedious obligations; for whom family is a source of pain, anxiety or regret. Such faith will not create perfect communities, or perfect love, out of the imperfect materials to hand (us, that is). But it does have power to draw us beyond our individual encounters with God, into expressing and communicating to others the love we have discovered – with the confidence that can only come through joyful Christianity. So the finding in the Temple sets before us an image of our lives – an interchange between perfect love and imperfect understanding, in our everyday experiences of being truly loved, though only partly understood. In meditating upon it, we move forward into the perfect love of God, in which we are wholly known and infinitely loved.

Centuries ago people objected to Christianity because it gave a positive value to the physical world and to human flesh on the simple grounds of the incarnation of Christ. Today, for the same reasons (science-based doubts about how God can work through the physical world) we might find the joyful mysteries hard to pray. This unease is a mindset from which Christianity challenges us to break free. Only through a transforming acceptance of the Holy Spirit who brings joy into the world, who *sanctifies* ordinary earthly things and makes them communicators of the message and meaning of God, can we finally lay hold of the joyful Christianity which is our birthright as children, and fellow heirs with Christ, of the same heavenly Father. No wonder that Christmas is for us the greatest celebration of the Christian year! For it reveals that 'the incarnation' is not a mysterious bit of jargon irrelevant to modern living, but the only thing which makes human life bearable, comprehensible, and, yes, *joyful* – as we find our abiding home in the divine presence.

A prayer for the finding in the Temple

God our Father,
your Son has promised us that if we seek you, we shall find
  you.
Guide our footsteps on the journey,
and bring us in time to our abiding home in your presence;
through the same, Jesus Christ our Lord. Amen.

Questions

1 Is Jesus ever rude or thoughtless?
2 If you can picture the scene of the finding in the Temple, how do you imagine the reactions to the 12-year-old Jesus?
3 Is it possible to balance the demands of family (or society) and self?
4 How does the finding in the Temple touch on your own life and experience of (a) family; (b) God?
5 Have you ever had to put your commitment to God before your commitment to your family or friends?

Final word

God's firstborn Son, the Word, descended into creation,
into everything that God had made,
and was put under its control,
so that all creation can seize hold of the Word
and ascend to him, surpassing the angels
and becoming the image and likeness of God.

Irenaeus, *Against Heresies* 5.36